Drink

Coca *(TRADE MARK REGISTERED)*

DELICIOUS an

Coca-Cola
answer to
no imitatio

Coca-Cola *qu*
in the public
holds it above

Pause . . .

refresh

Canada's Coca-Cola

Refreshing the Nation

for 120 Years

McClelland & Stweart

Library and Archives Canada Cataloguing in Publication

Hunter, Douglas, 1959-, author
    Coca-Cola anniversary book / Douglas Hunter.

ISBN 978-0-7710-2393-4 (hardback)

    1. Coca-Cola Company--History. 2. Coca-Cola Company--
History--Pictorial works. 3. Soft drink industry--Canada--History.
4. Soft drinks--Canada--Marketing--History. 5. Advertising--
Carbonated beverages--Canada--History. 6. Coca Cola (Trademark)
in art. I. Title.

HD9349.S634C63 2017   338.7'663620971   C2016-904586-2

Library of Congress Control Number is available upon request

Printed and bound in China
Photography credits can be found on page 145.
Book design by CS Richardson
Jacket photographs: © The Coca-Cola Company

McClelland & Stewart
a division of Penguin Random House Canada Limited,
a Penguin Random House Company
www.penguinrandomhouse.ca

1   2   3   4   5   21   20   19   18   17

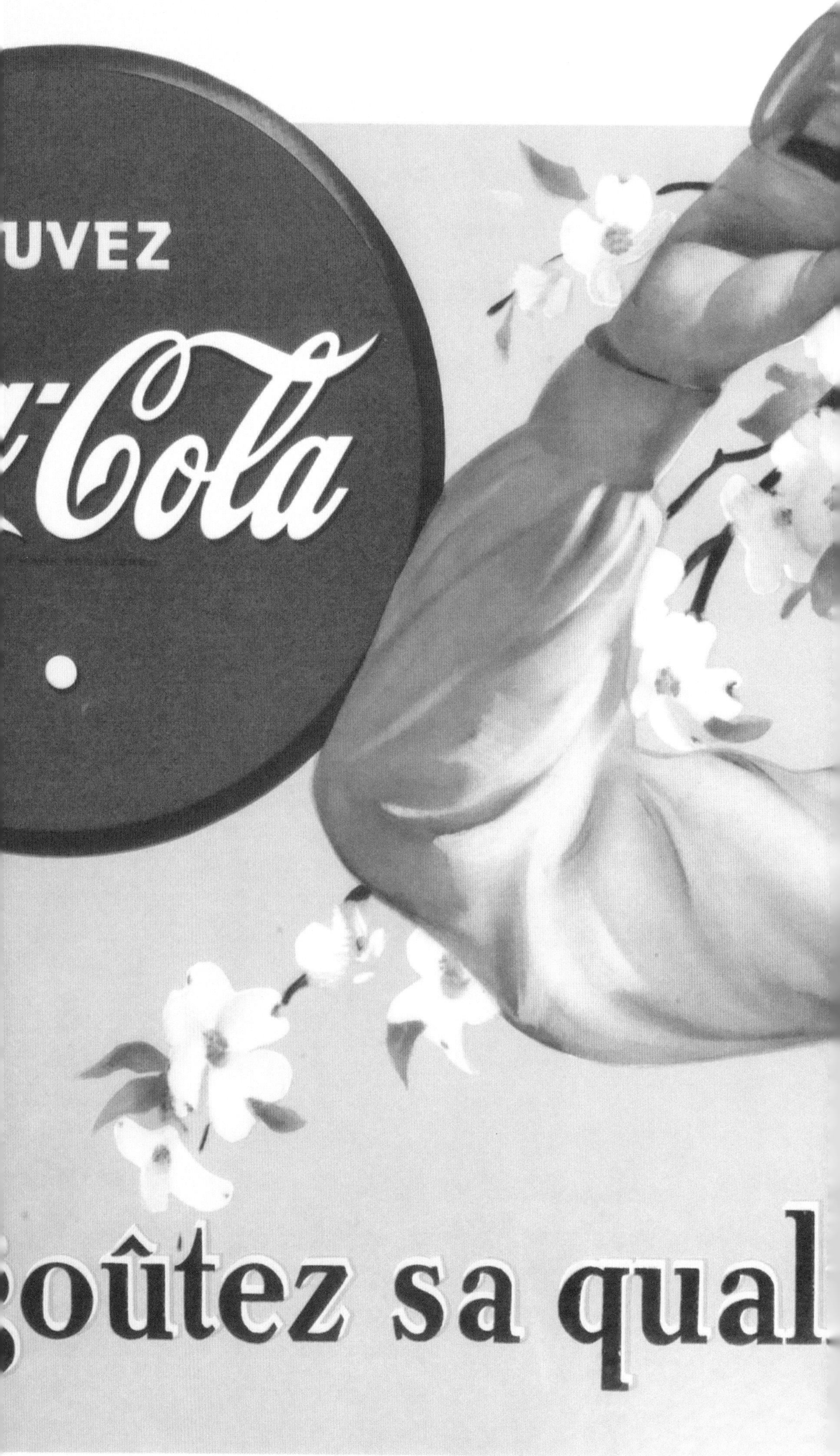
UVEZ
Cola
goûtez sa qual

A letter from the Associates of
Coca-Cola Canada

As Canada celebrates 150 years this year, we reflect on the great relationship Coca-Cola and Canada have had since 1897. For 120 years, Canadians have had a passion for the brand – after all, Coca-Cola and Canada share the same colours: red and white.

This book is the story of how Coca-Cola came to establish itself in Canada. While Coca-Cola is a globally iconic brand, there are parts of the Coca-Cola story that are distinctly Canadian.

Through extensive research of archived records and conversations with long-standing associates, this book shares the historic "made in Canada" secrets and encourages you to rediscover some of the important moments of Canada's evolving multiculturalism and diverse society.

Coca-Cola steadily developed a passion with consumers by listening to their expectations. Always within arm's reach of desire, at a sporting event or at a concert, Coca-Cola strived to share the emotions and the highlights of its story to become a great brand in today's pop culture – embedded in Canada's most historic moments.

Today, Coca-Cola employs over 6,300 Canadians and operates over 60 facilities across Canada as well as six manufacturing plants, operating a nationwide network that is able to serve Canadians in every province and territory. It's no wonder that Coca-Cola stands today as Canada's favourite brand of soft drink.

Finally, this book is a tribute to thousands of collaborators and partners who have helped build our success in this great country. We look forward to refreshing Canadians for the next 120 years and beyond.

Drink

Coca-Cola

TRADE MARK
REGISTERED

Delicious
and
Refreshing

THE COCA-COLA COMPANY   TORONTO—WINNIPEG

Beginnings

1897–1923

We don't know who served the first glass of Coca-Cola in Canada. We don't know the location of the soda fountain or from where in the United States its proprietor got the syrup that was transformed with soda water into the distinctive fizzy beverage that had been invented in Atlanta, Georgia, by John Stith Pemberton in 1886. We also don't know the name of the first Canadian customer to take a careful sip of the refreshment made from a secret recipe that would become the world's most popular soft drink. We do know that in 1892, Seth Fowle and Sons of Boston acquired sales rights for Coca-Cola in the New England states, as well as in New Brunswick, Nova Scotia, Prince Edward Island, and Newfoundland. But whether the Bostonians ever sold an ounce of Coca-Cola in Canada is a mystery.

We do know that Coca-Cola was definitely in Canada 120 years ago, in 1897. In a letter to shareholders in the sixth annual report, of 1898, recounting the company's performance in 1897, president Asa Candler wrote: "Coca-Cola is now sold to some extent in every state and in almost all the cities of the United States, and in some of the cities in Canada, and in the city of Honolulu, H.I."

But where in Canada was it being sold? Maybe the first thirst was quenched in Windsor, Ontario. One story has a syrup wholesaler or jobber fulfilling orders from Detroit for soda fountains there. Or maybe it was Toronto, where a soda fountain first served drinks made from the American syrup. Wherever the border crossings happened, they kept happening. In 1900, Charles Howard Candler, son of Coca-Cola owner and president Asa Candler (who would become Coca-Cola's president in 1916), visited Vancouver and Victoria to see if the company should start shipping syrup there. Charles

(Opposite) In this early promotional item, dated to 1914, a woman poses with a Coca-Cola bottle. Sales in Canada had been reported by the company since 1897. (Above) This 1918 trolley sign displays Coca-Cola as a registered trademark in Canada.

reported he was "favourably impressed and particularly delighted to find Coca-Cola on sale in both cities, since it had been imported directly by dispensers from Seattle jobbers and was being sold at 10 cents a glass." Because of customs duties, that price was double what Americans were paying for the drink.

Coca-Cola had entered the bottling age in 1899, and by 1905 the company had decided the demand from America's northern neighbour was enough for it to start bottling the drink in Canada as well, using syrup from the United States. In October 1905, the company applied to register the Coca-Cola trademark in Canada, and for $5,000 set up a small factory at 65 Bellwoods Avenue in Toronto, between Queen Street West and Dundas Street West, near Trinity Bellwoods Park. The trademark registration was granted in November, and in January 1906, the plant was up and running. Coca-Cola was bottling for the first time anywhere outside the United States.

The first known advertisement in Canada appeared in a newspaper in Peterborough, Ontario, in 1906. A local business, T.H. Hooper, ran an ad promoting "Cocoa Cola, the new drink that is so extensively advertised by us. Have a glass next time you pass." As Coca-Cola itself spent $4,392.57 on Canadian advertising that year, there were many more notices, which also properly spelled the product's name. Half of the company's 1906 advertising budget went to ads in newspapers and magazines, while the other half supported outdoor and street-car advertising. As in the United States, some ads promoted the drink as an alcohol-free temperance beverage. Word spread fast, and so did demand. John Lucas was the proprietor of the Grand Central Hotel, a main-street fixture in Haliburton, Ontario,

"Have a glass next time you pass." The first known Canadian ad for Coca-Cola appears in 1906 in Peterborough, Ontario.

From
the Home
of
Coca-Cola

into Canadian homes and stores. Ask your dealer to deliver a case of delicious, refreshing, pure and wholesome Coca-Cola at your home.

Demand the genuine by *full* name—halfnames and nicknames encourage substitution.

THE COCA-COLA CO., Toronto, Ont.

Call us on the Telephone

MADE IN CANADA

65 Bellwoods Avenue **Coca-Cola's first Canadian bottling plant opens in a working-class neighbourhood of downtown Toronto. The building still stands.**

which catered to summer vacationers, and in August 1906 he tried to order five cases. "We regret that, owing to the extreme rush of business at our factory we find it impossible to fill your order at the present time," the Toronto office informed Lucas. The Grand Central Hotel would have to be happy with two cases for the time being.

The general manager of Coca-Cola's new Canadian operation, Charles Albert Matson, arrived in Toronto from the United States as a full-time resident with his wife, Jeannette, in November 1906. Born in December 1867—five months after Canadian Confederation—Matson was more than six feet tall, without children to distract him, and in constant motion. The Matsons set up house a few doors from the factory on Bellwoods Avenue, and in the 1911 Canadian census Charles indicated he was working sixty hours a week, fifty weeks a year, for Coca-Cola in Canada.

Coca-Cola proved to be an un-stoppable Canadian success. Wherever Matson introduced the drink, customers wanted more of it. By 1908, sales of Coca-Cola bottled in Toronto were being recorded in Ottawa, Quebec City, and Montreal. On April 1, 1909, a small bottling plant was opened in Montreal, on the corner of Aylmer and Sherbrooke. A month after the plant opened, Matson reported that one salesman with a wagon had brought in almost $25 (about $500 today) in cash sales in one day. "This is in the face of extremely bad weather and almost new territory," Matson stressed, adding that the demand in Montreal was "really surprising." In 1910 business was so good that Matson had to move the plant to a larger location, on Rue St-Paul.

In these early days, Coca-Cola reached the Canadian customer in two ways. Coca-Cola had been invented as a soda-fountain drink, but by bottling it,

J.L. Brissette Coca-Cola forged one of its longest-lasting relationships in Canada with the bottler J.L. Brissette in Sainte-Agathes-des-Monts, in the Laurentian Mountains northwest of Montreal. In 1911, at age twenty-two, Jean-Louis Brissette had started his own soft drink company with $129—$128 to buy bottles, equip-ment, and flavour ingredients, and the remaining dollar to buy 20 pounds of sugar. Quebec's first Coca-Cola bottling facility at Rue Aylmer and Rue Sherbrooke in Montreal (above) had opened to fulfill demand for the beverage in Quebec in 1908. In 1916, Coca-Cola contracted J.L. Brissette as its exclusive bottler and distributor in the Laurentians. While no longer in the bottling business, J.L. Brissette continues to serve as a regional distributor in Quebec for Coca-Cola brands.

Drink trays were one of Coca-Cola's earliest forms of promotional item, and are highly sought by collectors.

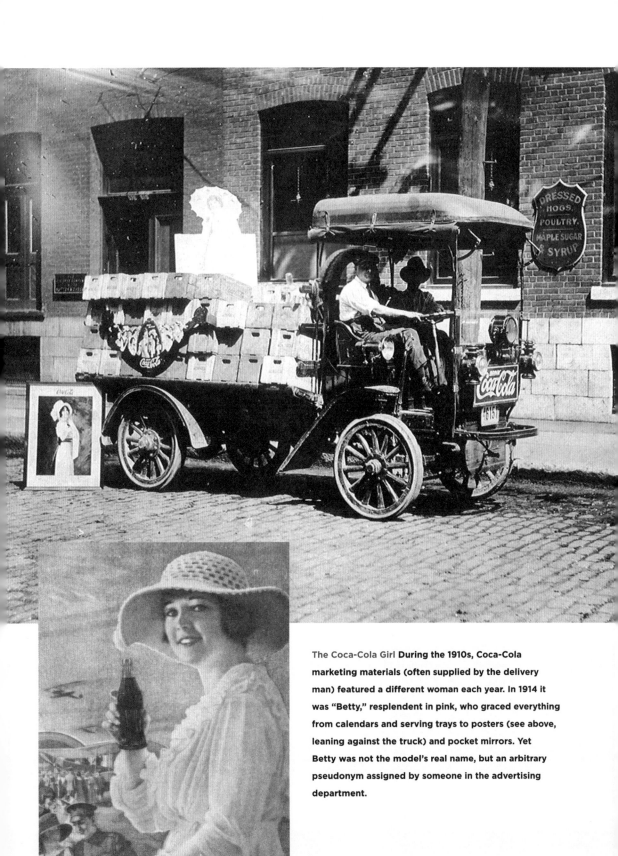

The Coca-Cola Girl **During the 1910s, Coca-Cola marketing materials (often supplied by the delivery man) featured a different woman each year. In 1914 it was "Betty," resplendent in pink, who graced everything from calendars and serving trays to posters (see above, leaning against the truck) and pocket mirrors. Yet Betty was not the model's real name, but an arbitrary pseudonym assigned by someone in the advertising department.**

I feel safe in saying that fully Nine Hundred Thousand people had their attention drawn to the fact there is at least one enterprising firm doing business in Canada.

Sales rep D.R. Leary reporting on Coca-Cola's brand exposure during the CNE, Toronto, 1909

the drink could be shipped and sold in any market. Even with the rise of bottling, soda fountains remained the dominant way customers consumed Coca-Cola for decades, and Canadian soda fountains dispensed Coca-Cola using syrup imported from the United States. Customers otherwise bought Coca-Cola in single bottles. The company was beginning to encourage home consumption, with Canadian ads that invited consumers as well as retailers to order wooden cases, which contained twenty-four bottles, right from the bottling plant. By 1908, Coca-Cola was also bottling and selling a ginger ale in Canada under the Gold Seal label, which would become a full product line of flavoured soft drinks in 1923.

In addition to the two company bottling plants in Toronto and Montreal, there were also six licensed or franchise bottlers in Canada soon after the Montreal plant opened. Matson proposed it would not be long before Coca-Cola was as popular in Canada as it was in the United States. There was only more good news to report in August 1909, after Matson travelled through New Brunswick and other parts of eastern Canada. The sale of Coca-Cola was "showing remarkably good increase in the Dominion."

Later that summer, Coca-Cola made a splash at the Canadian National Exhibition (CNE) in Toronto, which ran from late August to mid-September. Matson and one of his Toronto salesmen, D.R. Leary, plastered the CNE with Coca-Cola signage. As Leary reported: "Every Street, Corner, Booth and Lunch Stand had as many Coca-Cola signs as they could place to good advantage, a great deal of special work was done and fully half of the booths displayed nothing but Coca-Cola signs. The special work created a great deal of favorable comment,

COCA COLA SYRUP READY FOR SHIPMENT.

and the remark that 'every where you go you see Coca-Cola' was quite general. Everyone that visited the grounds saw a Coca-Cola Sign, and as the Fair was open Fifteen Days I feel safe in saying that fully Nine Hundred Thousand people had their attention drawn to the fact there is at least one enterprising firm doing business in Canada."

That September, William Taylor and John Corbett Pringle, who made soda water in Owen Sound and Sault Ste. Marie as Taylor & Pringle, visited the Toronto plant. Taylor & Pringle was creating a small empire of bottling operations in Ontario: by around 1911, it would have additional plants in Haileybury, Elk Lake, New Liskeard, Sudbury, and the Porcupine district around Timmins. Taylor & Pringle signed a bottling contract for the territory around Georgian Bay.

Trucks were purchased for deliveries in Toronto and Montreal in 1912, and the bottling contracts kept coming. Bottling started in Ottawa under J.J. Riley in 1912. That same year, a Finnish immigrant, Ed Faure, began bottling Coca-Cola in Port Arthur (now part of the city of Thunder Bay), Ontario. In his first year in business, Faure bottled 1,336 gallons. By late July in his second year, Faure was fast approaching 1,200 gallons. *The Coca-Cola Bottler*, a publication founded by the company in 1909, called Faure "an all-'round hustler." That same summer, George Kiefer secured bottling rights in Ridgeway, Ontario, across the border from Buffalo, New York, to please the estimated two hundred thousand Americans that flocked to Ontario's beaches along Lake Erie every summer. By early 1914, a bottler was in place in Hamilton, Ontario.

The big breakthrough came in Winnipeg. Coca-Cola began building a bottling plant in 1914, with some difficulty during the opening year of the First World War. Charles Matson moved to Winnipeg in

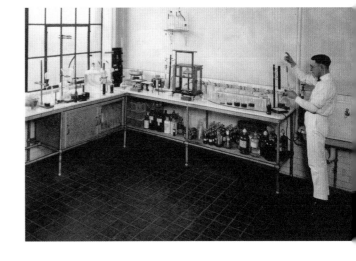

(Opposite) Coca-Cola barrels are ready for shipment in this unidentified Canadian factory. Syrup production began in Canada in 1923. (Above) A laboratory in an unidentified Canadian factory in the 1920s.

Coca-Cola employees in the recreation room of an unidentifed Canadian facility in the 1920s.

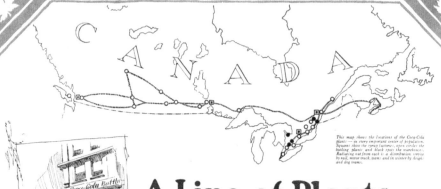

This map shows the locations of the Coca-Cola plants — in every important center of population. Squares show the syrup factories; open circles the bottling plants and black spots the warehouses. Radiating out from each is a distribution service by rail, motor truck, team; and in winter by sleigh and dog teams.

A Line of Plants from Quebec to Vancouver

Stretching out from east to west along the line of the Canadian Pacific, the trans-continental railway which first bound the scattered provinces of Canada into one great Dominion, Coca-Cola syrup factories, bottling plants and warehouses are a truly national manufacturing and distribution system.

The first plant was established in Toronto into 1901— 22 years ago. Now there are four syrup factories, twenty-one bottling plants and five warehouses—a distinct Canadian industry representing an investment of several million dollars, and handled by a Canadian organization with supplies purchased from Canadian sources.

This system is a service which is simply the natural outcome of Canada's recognition of the goodness and purity of Coca-Cola — a beverage made wholly from pure products from nature, prepared in absolutely sanitary plants with a finished art that comes from a lifetime of practice.

Thirst knows no season — no climate — no race — no creed. Wherever people are at work or at play across this broad land, Coca-Cola's system of supply provides the delicious and refreshing answer to thirst.

Sold everywhere —in bottles and at fountains.

Drink

Coca-Cola

TRADE MARK REGISTERED

Delicious and Refreshing

Our Manufacturing and Distribution System

Syrup Factories—Toronto, Montreal, Winnipeg and Vancouver.

Bottling Plants—Quebec, Montreal, Ottawa, Kingston, Belleville, Peterboro, Toronto, Hamilton, London, Windsor, Port Arthur, Winnipeg, Brandon, Regina, Saskatoon, Moose Jaw, Calgary, Edmonton, Lethbridge, Vancouver and Nanaimo.

Warehouses—Smith's Falls, Cornwall, Orangeville, Kitchener and Brantford.

THE COCA-COLA COMPANY
Toronto, Montreal, Winnipeg, Vancouver

late March 1915 and stayed for six months, in the process relocating the head office for Canadian operations; it would remain in Winnipeg until 1923. When the new enterprise opened to the public in April 1915, some two hundred businessmen visited to see what the fuss was about. The plant quickly proved not to be big enough, and was expanded in 1917. It still wasn't big enough, so the capacity was doubled in 1919. By then, Coca-Cola was overrunning western Canada. (And bear in mind that Saskatchewan and Alberta had only entered Confederation in 1905.) Coca-Cola had a second Manitoba bottling plant, in Brandon, by 1919. There were three plants in Saskatchewan, in Regina, Moose Jaw, and Saskatoon. Alberta had three plants, in Calgary, Lethbridge, and Edmonton, and British Columbia had a plant in Vancouver. Back east, the company now operated plants in Ottawa and Hamilton, as well as Toronto and Montreal, in addition to contracting with numerous licensed bottlers.

Coca-Cola experienced a much different relationship with its franchise bottlers in Canada than in the United States. In the United States, territorial bottling rights were secured by franchisees that then assigned the actual bottling to local bottlers. In Canada, the company contracted directly with bottlers, forging relationships that in some cases lasted for generations of family operators. The bottlers often were community anchors, a source of full-time and summer student employment, a place to tour with a school, Scout, or Guide group. Even the company-owned bottling plants, for many decades, were small operations compared to today, located in urban centres. Some, with street-front windows, allowed people to watch the bottling process. The franchise bottlers were small-business people, active in their local

In Canada, the company contracted directly with bottlers, forging relationships that in some cases lasted for generations of family operators. The bottlers often were community anchors, a source of full-time and summer student employment, a place to tour with a school, Scout, or Guide group.

A 1923 print advertisement shows the network of Coca-Cola factories, bottling plants, and warehouses in the year Robert Woodruff became company president.

communities in charitable and volunteer work, as were local plant managers. That meant Coca-Cola established a close relationship with communities large and small, at the grass-roots level, virtually from the beginning of its bottling efforts in Canada (see Chapter 8: The Community Bottler).

The success of Coca-Cola in Canada was nothing short of astonishing. Coca-Cola had also begun bottling in the Philippines and Cuba in 1909, and in Guam and France (in Paris and Bordeaux) in 1919, but Bordeaux did not last and Canada overwhelmingly was Coca-Cola's main international operation. Canada was even beginning to assist in international expansion. J.A. McAlpine, a bilingual Coca-Cola salesman in Montreal, was sent to Paris to help set up the new licensed bottling operation, which kept him busy for eighteen months. On his return, he was given the management of a new company plant in Quebec City.

By 1921, the Winnipeg plant was bottling more Coca-Cola than Atlanta and Birmingham, Alabama, combined. That year, three of the five bottling operations the company owned outside the United States were in Canada.

Winnipeg was bottling 4,000 gallons a day, while Montreal was bottling 3,000, gallons and Toronto 2,000 gallons. The other two international plants, in Cuba, trailed at 1,250 and 625 gallons. A plant in Peterborough was opened in early 1923. It was time to start making syrup in Canada as well, and production was under way in Montreal, Toronto, and Winnipeg in 1923—a landmark year, as a separate company, the Coca-Cola Company of Canada, Ltd., was incorporated on September 29, 1923. Head office was moved that October to a new facility at 90 Broadview Avenue in Toronto's east end. The three-storey facility featured offices, a convention hall, syrup production, and a bottling operation that could produce up to six thousand cases a day. That November, William Mongo Brownlee arrived in Toronto as managing director of the new Canadian company. The forty-four-year-old Atlantan left the presidency of the Cable Piano Company, a retailer he had built from one outlet in 1912 to nine when he made his career change.

Coca-Cola itself had just experienced a major change. An investment group led by Atlanta's Ernest Woodruff had acquired the company from the Candler family in 1919. In April 1923, Ernest Woodruff's son, Robert, was elected company president. He was also named the president of the Canadian subsidiary when it was incorporated that September. It was Robert Woodruff's vision, and to a great and even surprising degree the lessons delivered to him in Canada, that would define Coca-Cola's rise as a global brand and company over the coming decades.

Go North Young Man Robert Woodruff is elected Coca-Cola's worldwide president in 1923. He learned the ropes running the company's Canadian operations.

DESIGN.

A. SAMUELSON.

BOTTLE OR SIMILAR ARTICLE.
APPLICATION FILED AUG. 18, 1915.

48,160.

Patented Nov. 16, 1915.

FIG. 1.

The Contour Bottle In 1915, Coca-Cola introduced the most iconic element of its brand, after its script logo: the contour bottle. Until then, Coca-Cola bottlers had used a variety of straight-sided bottles. Harold Hirsch, the company's lawyer, argued for a distinctive design, recognizing that the bottle could be as much of a brand identifier for consumers as the label they glued to it—especially as labels tended to come off bottles that retailers kept chilled in tubs of ice. A bottle that was instantly recognizable not only to the eye but also to the hand, and even if broken into pieces, would help distinguish Coca-Cola from its competitors, especially from imitators that were using some variation of "Cola"

in their name. Straight-sided bottles were already being made with the Coca-Cola logo moulded into the glass, but when the same identification strategy was applied to a contour shape, there was no mistaking a "Coke" (a slang term the company discouraged until 1942) when it was in your hands.

The original contour, or "hoopskirt," bottle (later called the "Mae West") was created by the Root Glass Company of Terre Haute, Indiana, which secured a patent on November 16, 1915. In 1919, Coca-Cola decided to introduce the bottle design to Canada as well. As the distinctive contour shape was being used in Canadian advertising in 1919, it seems American bottles were used initially. The Dominion Glass Company of Montreal was contracted to produce at least twenty-five thousand for 1920. Root Glass worked with Dominion Glass to create the Canadian production version, and the bottle was registered in Canada as an industrial design on January 29, 1920. The 6.5-ounce bottle's shape would be tweaked over time, but until the introduction of "king size" bottles (10 ounces and larger) in the 1950s, this contour bottle, with its 5-cent price, was the one and only way Coca-Cola was sold, in Canada and throughout the world.

1899–1902

1900–1915

1915

1957

1961

Thirst
Knows
No Season

1923–1939

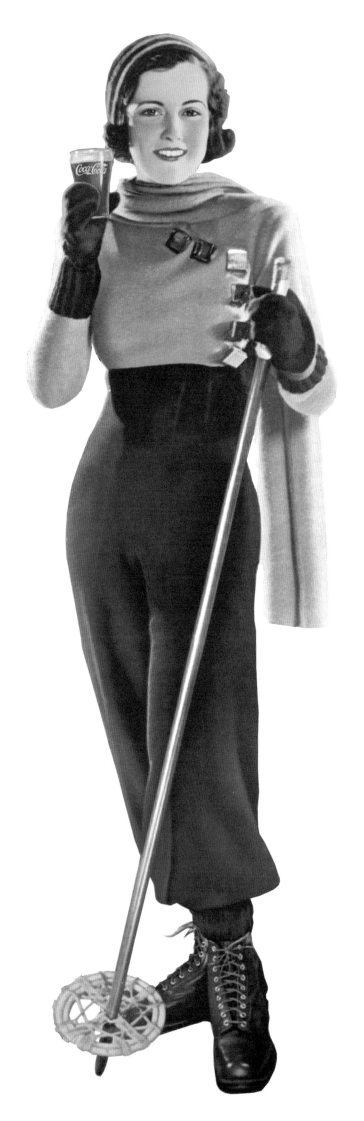

In the winter of 1923–24, Robert Woodruff embarked on a tour of Coca-Cola's Canadian operations. Woodruff was not only the president of the new Coca-Cola Company of Canada but he was also the new president of its parent, the Coca-Cola Company. What is more, Woodruff was new to soft drinks. He had no background in the beverage industry. When his father, Ernest Woodruff, organized the purchase of Coca-Cola for an investment group in 1919, Robert Woodruff was making his own way in life as a highly successful salesman for the White Motor Company in Cleveland. He had risen to White Motor's vice-presidency and had to take a pay cut to accept the Coca-Cola presidency in April 1923. But Woodruff was a quick study, and in Canada he grasped a basic fact about Coca-Cola that had never quite taken hold at head office in Atlanta during the Candler years.

As Woodruff told a Los Angeles newspaper reporter in February 1924 after concluding his swing through western Canada, he had been standing in a train station in Moose Jaw, Saskatchewan, when he noticed many fellow passengers were drinking Coca-Cola. That people in Moose Jaw were drinking Coca-Cola wasn't surprising. The southern Saskatchewan town of about nineteen thousand had a modern plant, with a thirty-two-spout bottle filler, and Coca-Cola was sold locally at soda fountains as well. *The Coca-Cola Bottler* in July 1922 had reported a major single order at the plant for one thousand cases, or twenty-four thousand bottles. "It was for immediate delivery and for cash. A solid carload as a retail order is SOME order, boys. Who can match this one?"

What surprised Woodruff is that people were drinking his product in impressive quantities when it was 35°F below zero outside.

(Opposite) A woman on skis enjoys a soda-fountain glass of Coca-Cola on the cover of the February 1933 issue of The Red Barrel. (Above) This syrup label was used from 1937 to 1941 at manufacturing plants in Toronto, Halifax, Vancouver, Montreal, and Winnipeg.

There's nothing small about cold weather on this side of the line. When we have cold weather, we are handed the genuine article.

The Coca-Cola Bottler, 1909

Coca-Cola, like other carbonated beverages that had been appearing in the United States since the early nineteenth century, was supposed to provide relief from the heat of summer. It was best known as a drink of the American south when its popularity began to spread. Its marketing followed a longstanding logic: people drank hot drinks when the weather was cold, and cold drinks when the weather was hot. And yet here were people in Moose Jaw, consuming Coca-Cola in weather that could shatter thermometers.

The remarkable thing about Woodruff's sudden insight is that, almost since the beginning of Canadian bottling operations in 1906, items had appeared in *The Coca-Cola Bottler* that defied the idea Coca-Cola was only a hot-weather drink. D.R. Leary of the Toronto plant, in reporting on general manager Charles Matson's recent swing through western Ontario in search of new bottlers, noted in the November 1909 issue (with a sly wink to Coca-Cola's efforts to discourage cheap imitations): "Cold weather is with us again, and, you know, there is nothing small about the cold weather on this side of the line. When we have cold weather, we are handed the genuine article: no substitution, nothing that sounds like it, and nothing that is just as good: and it has the proper trade-mark, registered way below zero, too. But, with all that, the demand for Coca-Cola will not let up. The people simply will have it: and that is what we are here for, to see that they get it. They know a good thing when they see it, and are sure of it when they taste it. There is one good feature about this cold weather, too, and that is that it keeps our goods 'on ice' and ready to serve. That counts a whole lot with a good bottle of Coca-Cola, for it wants to be ice-cold. So, you see, cold weather has its virtues, after all."

A female figure skater enjoys a Coca-Cola while resting. This image was used in advertising and on a serving tray in 1941.

Thirst
knows
no season

Drink
Coca-Cola

5¢

The Coca-Cola Company
Atlanta, Ga.

There were more reports like this in *The Coca-Cola Bottler* as the drink's popularity skyrocketed in Canada. "Some of the bottlers of Coca-Cola seem to think that in order to sell Coca-Cola they must have a territory where the sun is always hot and the snow never falls," the publication noted in September 1913, in sharing the success of Ed Faure as a bottler in Port Arthur, Ontario. "When these bottlers fall down on the job they blame it on the climate. More often than not these same bottlers would have fallen down under any other conditions." There was more of the same in the February 1914 issue, after Paul Arnoldi of Ottawa and W.M. McKinnon set up a bottling operation in Hamilton: "They have put in up-to-date machinery and are hustling for business, in spite of the fact that the thermometer in that section has been registering as low as 36 below *zero*. Think of it, you bottlers with cold feet."

In 1921, Coca-Cola did make a significant change in its marketing by introducing a new slogan, "Thirst Knows No Season," in an effort to expand sales outside the dominant summer season. The Christmas holiday period was the main target, and it is safe to say that the company was not planning an all-out drive to make Coca-Cola a rival to hot cocoa when the snow lay thick around potential customers. It took Robert Woodruff's arrival, as a new president and a newcomer to soft drinks, to grasp what was happening in Moose Jaw and other Canadian locations, and for the company to make Coca-Cola truly a thirst-quencher for all seasons.

Soon after Robert Woodruff concluded his 1923–24 tour of the Canadian operations, Coca-Cola's promotions were energized not just by Christmas but also by the idea of winter. Materials began to feature winter recreational themes, with

Coca-Cola Invents the Six-Pack **In 1923, Coca-Cola revolutionized beverage sales with the introduction of the six-bottle carton, which was patented in 1924. Until then, customers either bought 6.5-ounce bottles (the only way Coca-Cola was bottled until after the Second World War) for a nickel each from a retailer, or for a dollar could receive direct from the factory a wooden crate of two-dozen bottles. With the six-pack, which retailed for 25 cents, bottles could now be bought at a retail store in quantities that someone doing household shopping (as promotions emphasized) could easily carry. Coca-Cola also began selling bottles through retailers with reusable cartons. By 1940, the home-delivery service of crates of twenty-four was all but replaced by carton and six-pack sales at retailers.**

One of the earliest expressions of the "Thirst knows no season" slogan was this advertisement in the The Saturday Evening Post in 1922.

This Glass
Increases Sales

It is the latest thing in fountain glassware — special in design — thin, clear as a crystal, easy to clean, and you can turn it over on a marble counter and it won't break or chip. Measure your syrup by the marker, then fill with ice-cold carbonated water and stir with a spoon 'til it foams — that's a drink your customers will praise.

You can buy it in any quantity from your jobber

You can pick up three glasses at a time to wash and the brims won't touch and run the risk of being chipped.

Serve **Coca-Cola** 5¢

Delicious and Refreshing

THE COCA-COLA CO., ATLANTA, GA.

The Fountain Glass Dispensing Coca-Cola at a soda fountain was a minor art form when Coca-Cola was still prepared by hand, and the company supplied fountains with glasses to ensure its drink was made and served properly. This early flared Canadian fountain glass from 1925 has a lower etched line to indicate how much syrup the soda jerk should use.

Patrons crowd the counter of a soda fountain serving Coca-Cola on Bloor Street in Toronto in this photograph dating from 1920.

skaters and skiers. The artwork for the January 1927 cover of the company's publication *The Red Barrel* featured a man in a sweater and tuque reaching from somewhere beyond the North Pole, over a frozen Canada, to clink glasses of Coca-Cola with a young woman in a bathing suit in the southern United States. The art was adapted to advertising and further modified for the Cuban market, placing the young woman on the Caribbean island.

Coca-Cola regularly used the ongoing success in Canada in the 1920s and 1930s to urge on American bottlers and fountain clients in much warmer climates to try harder outside their peak summer sales seasons. In an address to the Coca-Cola bottlers convention in Boston in 1925, executive vice-president Harrison Jones remarked, "If I told you I sat in a skating rink at nine o'clock at night, at Winnipeg, Canada, and saw 2400 bottles of Coca-Cola sold to people, with the temperature at 32 degrees below zero, what would you say? I have seen it sold under those circumstances. And you talk about Boston weather. We were at the Rotary Club today. A man got up and said, 'John Smith, Port Arthur, Canada,' and everybody applauded. There is a Coca-Cola plant at Port Arthur doing business. I have been right there with him."

At the New England bottlers meeting in February 1926, Donald Hawkes, Coca-Cola's regional manager at Montreal, entertained the audience with tales of his days as a Coca-Cola salesman in the "Canadian Northwest." He had once driven 40 miles with a truckload of Coca-Cola in western Canada with the thermometer at 52 degrees below zero. He had to use charcoal heaters to stop the cargo from freezing and was pleased to report he made the entire trip without losing a single bottle.

The Red Barrel cover art, 1927. Inset: adapted for the Cuban market.

JANUARY
15TH
1927

Quenching Thirsts in Lakehead Country When Coca-Cola executives wanted to persuade American bottlers that the slogan "Thirst Knows No Season" truly meant what it said, time and again they pointed to the bottling operation in Port Arthur, Ontario, now part of the city of Thunder Bay. The little plant, established in 1912, serviced a huge territory around northern Lake Superior, with its salesmen seeking and servicing clients in towns, lumber and mining camps, and beyond, wherever a thirsty citizen could be found. A remarkable collection of photographs from 1923 to 1928 in the Coca-Cola Archives preserves the efforts to deliver Coca-Cola everywhere and anywhere in Ontario's Lakehead Country during the Roaring Twenties.

Coming and going through Old Quebec
the touring thousands
pause and refresh themselves

SPRINGTIME again and the call of the open road! Old Quebec City, where everybody goes or wants to go. California and Oregon park with Georgia and Massachusetts to enjoy the *pause that refreshes*. Through rose-colored glasses of ice-cold Coca-Cola tinted tourists review one of the great joys of the long, long trail. Far, across the Dominion and in every city, town and hamlet in the U. S. A., there's no drink so easy to get, so popular and so surely refreshing. • • • And at home in office or workshop, along hot, crowded city streets, how cheerful this same pause.

THE BEST SERVED DRINK IN THE WORLD

LISTEN IN — Grantland Rice — Famous Sports Champions — Coca-Cola Orchestra — Wednesday, 10:30 to 11 p. m. E. S. T. — Coast to Coast NBC Network

NINE MILLION A DAY

(Above) As well as gracing the cover of the April 1930 issue of *The Red Barrel*, this illustration of Old Quebec was featured in advertising in *The Saturday Evening Post*. (Below) Canada reinforces the "Thirst knows no season" message in a 1927 advertisement.

Canada had become something of a soda fountain that dispensed endless stories of Coca-Cola being sold in the most hostile environments. One of those stories was filed by Albert H. Staton, the manager of syrup sales for the Canadian company. Staton was one of several men from the American south who were sent to Canada by Coca-Cola to learn the business in the 1920s and 1930s, worked under Eugene Kelly, who succeeded William Brownlee as managing director of Coca-Cola Canada in 1926, and rose to the highest levels of the company (see Chapter 3: Kelly's BoysTeam). Riding a train from Saint John, New Brunswick, to New Glasgow, Nova Scotia, in search of new bottling opportunities, Staton wrote (as *The Coca-Cola Bottler* reported in February 1929): "It is sometimes difficult to keep the bottled goods from freezing. Today I was at a bottler's plant and it was 25 degrees below zero outside. All his stock was piled around the stove so as to be good and warm when he started out. The cases are piled down in the deep bed of a sleigh, a small oil stove placed in with them, the whole covered by bearskin rugs and he is ready to start. . . . In closing I would just like to say that in spite of our difficulties, we still sell a little Coca-Cola—our Quebec Bottlers had an increase of 68% last year." One bottler with only twenty-two hundred people in his territory had sold forty-eight hundred cases, while another, in a town of less than five thousand, had sold thirty-three thousand cases. "We have lots of bottlers in Georgia, who won't beat this per capita much," Staton noted.

By the time Staton filed his report from the frozen Maritimes, Canada's thirst for Coca-Cola was close to a thing of legend. But there was no denying the bare facts. In 1927, only a year after a

Keep It Cool Coca-Cola Canada pioneered the development of an official Coca-Cola cooler as a boost to winter retail sales, wherever Coca-Cola was sold. Eugene Kelly, managing director of Coca-Cola Canada, was also a vice-president of the Coca-Cola Company, and he spearheaded the project, assisted by John C. Staton (brother of Albert, who had come to work under Kelly in Canada in the 1920s). John C. Staton was then with the company's engineering department in Atlanta, and would join Kelly in Canada in 1931 (see Chapter 3: Kelly's Team).

As Kelly told bottlers in 1929: "The cooler will help us to our transition from a seasonal to a year 'round basis. The hot weather no doubt stimulates many customers to buy. Without this stimulus in the winter, and with the goods out of sight, we are in a very poor merchandising position. With this cooler to remind the individual he is thirsty, winter business may be built up." Coca-Cola's licensed bottlers could buy the coolers and in turn sell them to retailers. "The winter business," he assured them, "is yours for the asking."

Kelly explained how they sold six hundred of a prototype in 1928 in one Canadian city (probably Montreal) "outright, all cash, before the middle of June.

Mr. King's boys in Toronto sold forty in October and thirty-seven in November—all for cash, with a bitter winter staring them in the face. On the whole, we are convinced that on the average, our business was doubled in the six hundred stores in which these coolers were installed."

The production version was made by Glascock Brothers of Muncie, Indiana. Kelly addressed the 1929 Western Coca-Cola bottlers convention in Kansas City, urging them to place orders. As *The Coca-Cola Bottler* of May 1929 reported: "Mr. Kelly was very firm in his conviction that the dealer who serves Coca-Cola without proper refrigeration is no better than a Biological Impossibility and needs to be told so by the bottler. After all the care exercised by the Coca-Cola Co. to collect and blend nine flavors from nine sunny climes it is impossible to liberate them without the 10th flavor, REFRIGERATION." The cooler was in fact an icebox, not a refrigerated compartment. Nevertheless, along with the bell-shaped Coca-Cola fountain glass, the standardized, open-top retail cooler created by Kelly and his team in Canada was one of two significant innovations for Coca-Cola in 1929.

Coca-Cola without proper refrigeration is no better than a Biological Impossibility.

The Coca-Cola Bottler, 1929

Truly Thirst Knows No Season!

The "Coca-Cola Dog Team" in front of the Quebec Plant. Standing by the panel body car is Mr. A. Levesque, Coca-Cola branch manager at Quebec City.

Entry in Quebec Dog Derby Carries Coca-Cola Advertising Over Snow-Packed Course

When eleven drivers "mushed" their teams out on February 22nd for the greatest race in the history of the Eastern International Dog Sled Derby, over a 121-mile course, Coca-Cola of course was along.

O. Carrier handled the team pulling a sled which carried Coca-Cola advertising throughout the three-day race, in which the contestants covered more than forty miles each day. Prizes of $2,150 together with gold and silver trophies were awarded at a costume ball held in Chateau Frontenac on the night after the race.

"The Coca-Cola team carried our advertising throughout the race and of course, their driver, O. Carrier, re-

[2]

"Truly Thirst Knows No Season!" Dogsled racing was so big as a spectator sport that it was included in the Winter Olympic Games Lake Placid 1932 as a demonstration sport. That February, Coca-Cola decided to sponsor an entry by Ovide Carrier in the three-day, 121-mile International Dog Sled Derby at Quebec City. Carrier's sled carried a Coca-Cola logo, and Carrier was seen refreshing himself with Coca-Cola along the route. Carrier didn't win the race, but Coca-Cola's eastern regional manager, A.M. Day, was delighted with the exposure Coca-Cola gained before the many spectators, especially as Carrier's team came down the Grand Allée to the finish in the city. "You may feel assured," he reported to readers of *The Red Barrel*, "that we made it our business to see that all of these thousands had an opportunity to refresh themselves with Coca-Cola from our dealers."

devastating fire, the manager of the Montreal plant joined Coca-Cola's 100,000 Club, in recognition of bottling 100,000 gallons in a single year, a year before a manager in New York City did. Toronto's plant manager joined the club in 1929. Business was so good in Winnipeg in 1928 that the company sold its plant and began to build a new two-storey facility—the third time the city's plant was expanded or replaced since 1915. In 1930, Montreal bottled 517,000 gallons—an astonishing fivefold increase since 1927—which made manager A.M. Day a charter member of Coca-Cola's Half Million Club. Only the New Orleans plant had bottled as much. When Robert Woodruff noticed that per capita sales of Coca-Cola were higher in Montreal than in Miami, a "Thirst Knows No Season" print advertising campaign was launched in the United States to encourage American consumers to try Coca-Cola beyond the summer months. Those ads favourably compared Canadian sales in general with California and Florida.

By 1934, the Montreal plant was the largest Coca-Cola producer in the world. Despite the Depression, sales in Canada grew steadily, proof that in hard times many people could still find a few cents for a treasured refreshment. Coca-Cola's Canadian sales almost doubled between 1932 and 1937, rising from about $4.3 to $8 million. At the same time, the business mix began to shift noticeably. In 1936, for the first time, Coca-Cola recorded more syrup sales to bottlers than to soda fountains in Canada. Where soda fountains had accounted for 62 per cent of syrup sales in 1932, bottling represented 59 per cent of syrup sales in 1937. During the same period, bottling revenues for the company's own plants had soared 85 per cent, for a product that was still selling for a nickel.

(Above) A beverage poster from 1930.
(Overleaf) The Bellechasse plant, Montreal. By 1934, it was the largest Coca-Cola producer in the world.

What you want is a Coke

To work refreshed

DRINK
Coca-Cola

7¢

Including Federal Sales and Excise Taxes

101X

When you take a mid-morning break,
make it a real break . . .
with delicious ice-cold Coca-Cola:

Authorized bottler of Coca-Cola under contract with Coca-Cola Ltd.

HAMBLY'S BEVERAGES
OSHAWA, ONTARIO   PHONE 3-2733

The Hambly Brothers Ernie and Harold Hambly were brothers who ran Hambly Carbonated Beverages, the local Coca-Cola bottler in Oshawa, Ontario. In 1926, they made an innovative arrangement with Colonel R.S. (Sam) McLaughlin, president of General Motors (GM) of Canada, to have Coca-Cola sold from roving trucks to GM's Oshawa workers. As one Coca-Cola executive in Atlanta remarked with admiration, "It's beginning to look as if these fellows in Canada have put something over on us."

Sam McLaughlin's family had founded the McLaughlin Motor Car Company, the forerunner of General Motors of Canada. The family had also been a pioneer in the Canadian soft drink industry. Sam's older brother John

had set up a plant in Toronto in 1889, creating a variety of sodas that included a ginger ale. In 1905, that ginger ale was patented as Canada Dry. After John's death, the surviving brothers, Sam included, took over the business, J.J. McLaughlin Ltd. In 1924, American interests purchased J.J. McLaughlin, including its Canada Dry assets. Two years later, Coca-Cola bottled by the Hambly brothers was being sold to Sam McLaughlin's auto workers in Oshawa.

When Oshawa's Bradley Arena burned down in June 1928, Ernie and Harold Hambly teamed up with Sam McLaughlin and several other partners to give the city a replacement that had few rivals in Canada. They began building Hambly Arena in October 1929, just as the stock market crashed to usher in the Great Depression, but they kept going, at an estimated cost of $100,000. The arena was completed in an amazingly short time, opening in January 1930. That same year, the Hambly brothers expanded their Coca-Cola bottling to Sarnia.

Hambly Arena (or Oshawa Arena) is sometimes said to have been the largest arena in Canada when it was built, but in seating capacity at least, the Montreal Forum, built in 1924 with room for ninety-three hundred, was larger. Still, Hambly Arena was a marvel. It could hold five thousand spectators (with seating for 3,750) and its innovative arched roof design eliminated support posts that interfered with sightlines. Its ice refrigeration system was state of the art, and players enjoyed comparatively sumptuous dressing rooms, with showers and baths. Naturally, Coca-Cola was served at its concession stands. It was home to the Oshawa Generals of Ontario junior hockey, who won seven straight OHA championships and three Memorial Cups (the national junior hockey championship) from 1937 to 1944. Unfortunately, like its predecessor, Hambly Arena burned down, in September 1953.

Canada's successes inspired executives within the greater Coca-Cola family to urge bottlers to reject the tired notion that Coca-Cola was only a summer drink. Ralph Powers of the Western Coca-Cola Bottling Co. in Chicago heralded Montreal's performance in an address at the Louisville Coca-Cola Conference in 1935. "If in the year 1920 the best informed Coca-Cola man on earth had been asked to make a guess as to where the largest Coca-Cola plant on earth would be in the year 1934, he would probably have guessed one of a number of large American cities, but certainly he would not have guessed right, because no reasonable man would have guessed Montreal, Canada." He also pointed out that the second-largest sales month for the plant consistently was December, not a summer month. (Coca-Cola Canada's Eugene Kelly would recall that in 1928, one of the Canadian plants had its second- and fourth-largest single-day orders in the month of December.) Furthermore, Powers proposed, if you were asked to name the North American city with the worst per-capita consumption, surely it would be Winnipeg, which was "two jumps this side of the North Pole." To the contrary, Winnipeg's per-capita consumption in the depths of the Depression in 1932, he revealed, was an impressive thirty-seven bottles.

Powers concluded with a rallying cry: "Fellows, I often think of this business of winter sales, especially in these more northerly states represented in this meeting, a battle with the forces of winter. . . . When the skies of December grow dark and the wind comes howling out of the north with snow in its teeth and the temperature goes down, down, down, and when we pick up the papers and read of the lovely weather they are having down along the Gulf Coast of Texas, Alabama and Mississippi, we are apt to think of ourselves as out in the front line trenches fighting a hard battle with the forces of winter. Sometimes we grow discouraged, but when we turn again to the front, we see far out ahead hundreds of miles in the direction of the enemy the flag of Coca-Cola, our flag planted upon the very parapets of the fortress of winter, all along the Canadian front, and that flag seems to say to us, 'This position has been captured. We have defeated the forces of winter in its own stronghold. It can be done. You of the northern states are no longer in the front-line trenches. The ground between belongs to you. Advance! Claim your own!'"

Just a drink---but what a drink!

Coca-Cola executives, 1925. Eugene Kelly (then vice-president for the central region) stands in the back row, second from right.

Kelly's Team

Drink

Coca-Cola

Delicious and
Refreshing

With the arrival in Toronto in January 1926 of Eugene (Gene) Kelly as the new managing director of Coca-Cola Canada, the Canadian company entered a remarkable period as an innovation centre and a proving ground for future leaders of the Coca-Cola Company worldwide. Canada set new standards in sales volume and plant operations while showing that Coca-Cola could be far more than a summer beverage. It also proved that Coca-Cola could be an international success.

Kelly had worked for Robert Woodruff at White Motor Company in Cleveland. When Woodruff arrived as president of Coca-Cola in 1923, he brought Kelly with him, at first putting him in charge of the company's central region at its Chicago office. "Tall, ramrod straight, he could still do one-handed pushups in his forties," Frederick Allen has written in *Secret Formula*. "With his clipped moustache and shock of salt white hair, he looked every inch the colonel he had been in the Great War."

Kelly was a brilliant and persuasive salesman, number-cruncher, and efficiency expert. As a vice-president of the Coca-Cola Company as well as the head of Coca-Cola Canada (rising to the Canadian presidency in 1934), he deserved much credit for turning a new advertising slogan of 1921, "Thirst Knows No Season," into a business reality. Typical of his attention to detail was how he carried a thermometer with him on his Canadian travels to prove that it was exactly 7.5 degrees warmer indoors in Canada in the winter than it was outdoors in the summer.

A glass Fahrenheit (-50 to 120 degrees) thermometer on a metal porcelain sign from 1939 confirms that Coca-Cola can be enjoyed in any climate!

"

Bottled Coca-Cola tastes best when consumed directly from the clean, sparkling, sealed bottle in which you receive it. It's easy and pleasant to do like this! . . .

Place the topmost sterile rim of the opened bottle lightly against your lips—avoid putting the neck of bottle in your mouth.

Now part your lips slightly to permit free entry of air into the bottle—avoid closing lips on bottle.

Then tilt your head and bottle together— Coca-Cola flows freely into your mouth. Drinking this way you can enjoy a sip at a time or as much as you please.

The distinctively-shaped Coca-Cola bottle is specially designed to fit the grip of your hand comfortably.

"

Eugene Kelly was such a stickler for detail and process that he even wrote instructions for how Canadians should drink Coca-Cola, which were illustrated with a Canadian worker and later published in *Coca-Cola Overseas* in 1952. (Overleaf) A revolutionary Coca-Cola innovation is the six pack. (See also page 29.)

THE BEST SERVED DRINK IN THE WORLD

A pure drink of natural flavors served ice-cold in its own bottle—the distinctive Coca-Cola bottle. Every bottle is sterilized, filled and sealed air-tight by automatic machines, without the touch of human hands—insuring purity and wholesomeness.

COCA-COLA BOTTLING COMPANY

Drink
Coca-Cola
Delicious and Refreshing

6 Bottles in
This Handy SIX-BOX

COCA-COLA BOTTLING CO.

A package
your family will give
a *real* welcome

As Allen has noted, Woodruff relied on Kelly in Toronto to train promising young men in the company's ranks. That meant many major figures who rose to the senior ranks of the Coca-Cola Company after the Second World War had spent their formative careers in Canada. And because he was also given charge of overseeing the company's European operations from Toronto in the early 1930s (as well as Cuba), Kelly was instrumental in making Coca-Cola an international success. Among his protégés was Ernest Brennan, who began working for Coca-Cola in Canada in 1927 and was transferred to Australia in 1938 to start bottling operations there. In 1949, Brennan would become Coca-Cola's district manager in New Zealand.

John Curtis Staton had joined Coca-Cola in 1925 with a bachelor's degree in electrical engineering from Georgia Tech. His first job was pure labour: painting barrels and unloading sugar. After also earning a law degree at night school in 1928, he worked in the company's engineering department in Atlanta. There, he helped Eugene Kelly in Canada develop the company's cooler in 1929, then joined Kelly in Canada in 1931. From 1931 to 1938, he served in succession as the manager of the central, western, and eastern regions of Canada, and married Jocelyn Botterell of Winnipeg. He was made manager of the Australasian region in 1938 (where Ernest Brennan had also just been sent from Canada), and would also head up operations in Brazil and New Zealand. He returned to America in 1948 with a senior position at Coca-Cola Export Corporation, and was named Coca-Cola's vice-president of manufacturing in 1948 as well as an assistant to the president in 1950.

H.B. Nicholson, who in 1952 became the first person to serve as president of the Coca-Cola

"Mr. Nick" H.B. Nicholson with his wife, Juliet, a Torontonian. They met during his first management assignment for the company in Canada.

Company after Robert Woodruff, came from a small town in Georgia. He had already been a lawyer, teacher, and businessman when he joined Coca-Cola in 1933. The company first sent him to New England to ride a route sales truck, then assigned him a management position in Canada. He met his wife, Juliet, in Toronto, and they married there in 1939. He was known as "Mr. Nick," otherwise as Baron of Balvanie, because of a castle he bought in Scotland while directing activities of Coca-Cola Export Corporation. Among the many senior positions Nicholson held, in addition to president of the Coca-Cola Company, was president of Coca-Cola Export and chairman of the board of the Canadian subsidiary, Coca-Cola Ltd. (as it became known in 1945).

John and Lee Talley were two brothers from Alabama who played major roles in the company's international success and spent their formative years in Canada under Eugene Kelly. Lee Talley joined Coca-Cola in 1923 and was made branch manager in Vancouver in 1927. He served as western and eastern regional manager and then vice-president of the Canadian company, marrying Marjorie Irene Moxam of Winnipeg before moving to New York in 1943 to serve as vice-president of Coca-Cola Export. In 1952, he became president of the Canadian operation, and additionally president of Coca-Cola Export in 1954. In 1958, Lee Talley became president of the Coca-Cola Company and chairman of the board in 1961. He told a bottlers association meeting in 1959: "I have made Bottler calls all the way from British Columbia to Bangkok, Bombay, Mombassa, Berlin, Buenos Aires and back again." In Canada, he explained, he learned the bottling side of the business, and was exposed to the overseas expansion managed by Kelly.

The Talley Brothers John (top) and Lee. Originally from Alabama, each married Canadian girls.

"There [in Canada] it was first impressed on me how this total business of ours—fountain, bottle, overseas—so completely fits together for the good of all."

Lee Talley's younger brother, John, came straight out of Duke University in 1934 to work as a fountain syrup salesman in Toronto. He was then a fountain and bottler representative in Winnipeg, the manager of the Canadian company's fountain division in Toronto, the manager of the Port Arthur plant, and then of the Windsor plant. He married Evelyne Hunter of Toronto. After transferring overseas as a technical observer during the Second World War (see Chapter 5: Wartime), John Talley managed Coca-Cola's southern European division. He was then sent to Australia in 1951 to oversee operations there, and in 1956 was made a vice-president of Coca-Cola Export and given charge of a newly created Mediterranean and Middle East Area, with headquarters in Rome.

With such ongoing success and a reputation for excellence in its Canadian operations, Coca-Cola found corporate leaders within Canada as well. Young men with university degrees were tapped to manage bottling plants and serve as salesmen. The most outstanding recruit was Ralph E. Sewell. He began his Coca-Cola career as a route salesman in 1934 after graduating from the University of Toronto. After a period as a special salesman and four years as a sales manager in the Toronto area, Sewell was appointed manager of the western region in 1940. He rose steadily through the Canadian operation and became its president in 1958. Sewell was elected chairman of the board in 1966 and served until retirement in 1974. During his postwar career, he was the dominant figure in the Canadian soft drink industry.

Homegrown Talent **Ralph Sewell (right) joined Coca-Cola as a route salesman after graduating from the University of Toronto. He served as chairman of the board from 1966 to 1974. He is pictured here with Grand Slam golf icon Gary Player.**

The Right Stuff. **A poster designed in 1928 for the Canadian market.**

Refresh yourself
טרינקט
Coca-Cola
TRADE MARK
עשמאק און דערפרישענד
RUDDY KESTER LTD

Kosher
Coca-Cola

NOTICE!

KOSHER LEPESACH FOR PASSOVE

Under the direct Supervision of Rabbi Kahanovit

THE PRICE REMAINS THE SAME

Order a case sent to your home

נאָטיס!

קאָקא-קאָלא ✡ כשר לפ

בהשגחת

הרב י. י. כהנאָוויטש

די פּרייז בלייבט די זעלבע ווי תמיד

ב' אדר, תר"ע, וויניפּעג.

מיר מאכן באקאנט אז דער קאָקאַ-קאָלא איז א ריינער וועדזשעטיבל געטראנק. אנאליזירט ביי די גרעסטע בעמיקער,
עס איז ריין פון א משהו חמץ, ספּעציעל נייע באטלס אויף פּסח. יעדער באטל קאָקאַ-קאָלא מיט א קאָרק כשר לפסח פון
ב כהנאָוויטש איז כשר לפסח בלי שום חשש. הרב כהנאָוויטש וויניפּעג

ארדערט א קיים פאר אייער היים

In the United States, the first kosher version of Coca-Cola appeared in Atlanta in 1935, under the guidance of Rabbi Tobias Geffen. But Canada had already been making kosher Coca-Cola for Passover for at least six years. In September 1929, a Coca-Cola bottler in Oakland, California, contacted Coca-Cola Canada, asking how it had arranged its kosher version for Passover. The short answer was: with a fair bit of organizing—even though the beverage's secret formula was never altered. The most notable part of Canada's pioneering effort with kosher Coca-Cola was the way the company stood by its Jewish customers during the frightening rise of Nazi power in Germany and outbursts of anti-Semitism at home.

Rabbis in Winnipeg and Montreal provided the hechsher certification for the syrup. An additional hechsher was required at plants in Canada in which kosher syrup was turned into bottled product. Kosher bottles at first carried a paper hechsher label, but in 1930 Coca-Cola began using special hechsher bottle caps for each Canadian city in which kosher approval was made. Cartons were also given special labelling. In 1930, a total of 16,686 kosher cases were produced in eastern Canada, with most of them (10,475) sold in Montreal. Another fifteen hundred were consumed in Winnipeg. In all, kosher Coca-Cola was sold that Passover in Montreal, Ottawa, Quebec, Toronto, Peterborough, Belleville, London, Windsor, and Hamilton in eastern Canada, and in Winnipeg, Brandon, Calgary, Regina, Vancouver, and Edmonton in western Canada.

In Montreal, the Jewish Community Council oversaw the kosher process for syrup and local bottling. In addition to the koshering cost, the community council collected the fee Coca-Cola paid to advertise

Kosher Coca-Cola was a Canadian innovation. Special bottle caps were used beginning in 1930, and flyers (opposite) were circulated in Jewish communities, in this case in Winnipeg.

FROM MATZOH TO MANDELEN

WE HAVE EVERYTHING for PASSOVER

Coca-Cola
Trade-mark ®

TaB Fresca
כשר לפסח

the Passover kosher version in the *Canadian Eagle* and the *Canadian Jewish Chronicle*. Coca-Cola also produced flyers in Hebrew to promote the kosher version.

The overall koshering cost varied from year to year, and had been as high as $350 in Montreal. In February 1934, Lee Talley met with the Montreal council to discuss the kosher program for the upcoming Passover. A future president of the Coca-Cola Company, Talley was then manager of Coca-Cola Canada's eastern region, whose office was in Montreal. Born in Monroeville, Alabama, in 1901, Talley had been with Coca-Cola since 1923, and had never been through a negotiation quite like this one. He did not resent the negotiating, as he understood the koshering funds were dedicated to charitable works. He reported to the Toronto office with some admiration (and amusement with his own performance): "I never saw such a trading proposition in my life. You go into a large room in which are seated around a long table a half dozen or so Jewish Community members who proceed to tell you all about your business and the value of Koshering and why you should pay much more than you are now paying and why there is no reason in the world for you to pay less."

The council surprised him by proposing a reduced fee of $200, then further surprised him with the condition that kosher sugar from the St. Lawrence sugar refinery in Montreal be used. Talley confessed to head office: "I am sorry now that my wits were so sluggish that I made a virtual acceptance of this condition." After the meeting Talley learned Coca-Cola had no provision for buying any additional sugar, as it already had a large quantity. When he informed the community council of the problem, it withdrew the kosher sugar request and stayed with the $200 expense, even though it had just lost the fee for any kosher sugar that would have been used.

From the mid-1930s onward, the expense and complexity of packaging the kosher product for different Canadian communities for a Passover period of about ten days made the program an annual source of debate within the company. Fewer cities appeared to ask to participate, but in the larger centres, demand increased. In 1937, sales increased by about one thousand cases over 1936 in both Ottawa and Winnipeg and were up 13 per cent in Montreal. In Toronto, which had required five thousand cases (which included sales to other southern Ontario cities) in 1930, sales had grown steadily, from 8,852 in 1934 to 11,593 in 1937, which included a 15 per cent increase in the past year. Whenever the head office in Toronto polled its plant managers in these main markets, they always argued for the koshering program.

By 1937, the reasons for continuing the program had acquired an additional dimension. As John C. Staton, the new eastern regional manager in Montreal, informed the Toronto office in 1937: "The Jewish people today are extremely sensitive of any action which even savours of discrimination." Coca-Cola already had been dragged into the virulent anti-Semitism that could erupt in Canada. In 1932, the publisher of three French-language community newspapers in Montreal began running a series of fiercely anti-Semitic articles, which among other things alleged Jews were commanded by the Talmud to kill Christians. One edition included a list of soft drink manufacturers that should be boycotted because they were 100 per cent Jewish-owned enterprises. Among them was Coca-Cola. Hebrew signage on

In early 1939, with Hitler inflicting fresh terrors on Jews and another world war imminent, the kosher Coca-Cola program in Canada could no longer be evaluated just on the basis of expenses and sales.

Coca-Cola's Montreal vehicles may have encouraged the idea that it was a Jewish company, but the assertion was part of a broad whisper campaign targeting the company in North America. Coca-Cola grappled with how to respond. The plant manager in Montreal advised legal action, but the Toronto office thought it best to ignore the allegation: "Usually sheets of this type are very skilful at twisting one's statements to serve their own ends. It is possible that should you deny that we are a Jewish firm they might publish it in such a manner that would offend our Jewish friends."

In Canada, the anti-Semitic campaign against Coca-Cola persisted. A Coca-Cola bottler in Trois-Rivières reported to the company that packages of pamphlets

were arriving every two weeks at Coca-Cola retailers, with six or seven different ones targeted in every mailing. The pamphlets charged that the caffeine in a 6.5-ounce bottle of Coca-Cola (which was about one-quarter to one-eighth of the amount in an eight-ounce cup of coffee) could be fatal and that the drink was being produced by a Jewish company. It was left to the reader to assume that Jews were trying to kill Christians with a soft drink.

In early 1939, with Hitler's Germany inflicting fresh terrors on Jews and another world war imminent, the Canadian kosher Coca-Cola program could no longer be evaluated annually just on the basis of expenses and sales. One of the strongest voices in favour of the kosher program was J.T. Singlehurst, a young Canadian executive who had made a rapid rise since joining Coca-Cola Canada as a syrup salesman in 1932. In 1936, he was

Refreshing In Any Language Trilingual delivery trucks, Montreal, circa 1937.

named western regional manager in Winnipeg. In January 1939, Singlehurst argued for the program to continue, citing a general sympathy among Christians toward the Jewish people "on account of more recent and violent persecutions in Europe." Any change in the kosher program could be seen as contributing to this discrimination and would harm Coca-Cola in the eyes of many consumers. A week later, the treasurer of the Coca-Cola Company wrote Eugene Kelly, president of Coca-Cola Canada, recommending he continue the kosher program: "The Regional Managers are unanimous in the opinion that it would be inadvisable to discontinue Koshered 'Coca-Cola' this year in view of the very aggravated situation in Europe and the sensitiveness of the Jewish people at this time."

The program continued, and kosher Coca-Cola is still made for the Canadian market.

At first, Kosher Coca-Cola bottles in Canada were marked with a paper label, before special caps were adopted.

Wartime

1939–1945

Your
thirst
takes
wings

Paus
Go refr

Coca-

The Second World War cast a long shadow over Canadian lives—in combat, on the home front, and well beyond the end of fighting, as the world tried to right itself. For Coca-Cola in Canada, the war meant employees enlisting in the military and wartime rationing in strategic or vital materials that threatened the continued production of all soft drinks. At the same time, Coca-Cola found a role in the war, as a refreshment beloved by workers in factories turning out munitions and weapons for the Allied cause, and by soldiers, sailors, and airmen, whether they were in training or in combat. Coke became one of those familiar comforts that reminded enlisted men and officers alike of life at home. While Coca-Cola's production was affected by rationing, it also became to a surprising degree part of the Allied war effort.

Rationing in strategic material, especially gasoline and rubber, affected the company (and its thirsty customers); without a reliable supply of fuel and tires for trucks, it was a challenge to deliver anything. The main restriction on the continued production of Coca-Cola was sugar rationing, although as it turned out, the impact wasn't really felt until 1944, when there was such a shortage that the Coca-Cola plant in Red Deer, Alberta, shut down completely. As a soft drink, Coca-Cola was also subjected to a special wartime excise tax that increased the price of a bottle by a penny—which was a 20 per cent increase. In 1945, sales in Canada fell 24 per cent in bottles and 27 per cent in syrup, and they didn't begin to recover until 1947.

There are too many Coca-Cola employees and bottlers who served in the war to recount. Norman Johnstone, to name but one, was a member of the Royal Canadian Air Force (RCAF) reserve when he joined the company as a special salesman with

(Opposite) An easel advertisement by the Coca-Cola Company of Canada Limited, lithographed in Canada in 1941.
(Above) A wartime hanging sign circa 1942 declares Coca-Cola's promise to all Canadians—soldiers, factory workers, and citizens at home alike—during World War II.

the Regina plant. When war broke out, he was called up for active duty, and he moved rapidly to the rank of squadron leader, leading Spitfires on raids across the English Channel. During one particularly busy action in November 1941 over Calais, Johnstone's squadron destroyed or damaged several German aircraft, with Johnstone himself damaging a Messerschmitt fighter. The action was so outstanding that Johnstone was mentioned in dispatches and was among twenty-four Canadian servicemen included in the King's honour list in January 1942.

One of the more unusual contributions to the war effort was made by Leo Couture, a young Québécois who had joined the Canadian Army in 1940 and would become a major figure in Coca-Cola bottling in Canada. An eye injury in hockey prevented him from serving overseas with his two brothers, but he rose to the position of staff-sergeant with the 22nd "Van Doos" regiment and gained lifetime fame for his accidental role in the top-secret Quebec Conference of British, Canadian, and American leaders in August 1943. Couture was one of only two members of the Canadian military with security clearance for the conference room. When the historic meeting between Canadian prime minister William Lyon Mackenzie King, British prime minister Winston Churchill, and American president Franklin D. Roosevelt was over, Couture was tidying the room when he found some documents in a drawer.

He took them home, thinking nothing of them, and only then realized they were detailed plans for the Normandy invasion in ten months. Couture turned them in and was sworn to secrecy about both their contents and who had committed the horrendous security breach. Many years later, after Couture's death, family members would say it

A Coke and a Smile **Canadian soldiers (and guests) at ease, 1943.**

was Churchill who had left the documents behind. At the second Quebec Conference in September 1944, Couture was awarded the British Empire Medal, without any official explanation as to why.

After the war, Couture became a leading citizen of Thetford Mines, Quebec, an astute businessman and philanthropist who held the local Coca-Cola bottling franchise. He was also a scout for the Montreal Canadiens and was instrumental in negotiating the contract that saw Jean Béliveau leave senior hockey and join the Canadiens in 1953. In October 1953, Béliveau married Couture's sister, Elise. Couture created a five-team junior hockey league in Thetford Mines and then operated junior A teams, including the Canadiens, that in the 1960s groomed a number of talents, including Réjean Houle, Gilbert Pereault, and Marc Tardif, for the National Hockey League. Couture was serving as president of the Canadian Soft Drink Association when poor health claimed him at fifty-two in 1972.

Coca-Cola proved to be one of those reminders of home considered crucial to service morale. A letter to Coca-Cola headquarters from an American who had enlisted in the Canadian Army and was awaiting D-Day in England underscored its importance.

"When I first went to Canada I noticed that the 'Coke' bottles there were white [actually clear], whereas in the States they are of a greenish hue," wrote Corporal D.L. Short. "Naturally, when I landed in this country it came to my notice that the bottles here were also white, but as in Canada, over here you spot a green one now and then. I was not long finding out that these bottles had the name of a city in one of our great United States on the bottom. Now it has become a game with most of our chaps when a green bottle is seen to look immediately on the

The Kenora Bottler Canadian bottlers continued to fascinate the greater Coca-Cola family with their seemingly endless ingenuity in getting the product to market in the Great White North. The February 1940 issue of the company's publication *The Red Barrel* profiled Kenora bottler A.S. Olson and his airborne efforts to deliver Coca-Cola to the farthest reaches of his territory, which included fly-in communities hundreds of miles north in places such as Sioux Lookout and the Uchi Lake region.

The Aboussafy Family Coca-Cola's licensed bottler in Mont-Joli, in the Bas-Saint-Laurent region of Quebec, was Royal Bottling Works. It was run by the Aboussafy family, whose members had arrived in the area from Syria and Lebanon before the First World War. Leo Aboussafy operated a monstrous truck/snowmobile (shown in 1939) in delivering Coke to customers. When the Second World War erupted, Royal Bottling continued to produce Coca-Cola (as an ad in *Le Progrès du Golfe* of August 22, 1941, shows), and the Aboussafy family gave generously to local Victory Bonds drives, but Leo was no longer on hand to get the bottle crates past the snowdrifts. A pilot before the war, Leo served as an armourer with 434 Squadron of the Royal Canadian Air Force. He appears in the far right of this photo (left) of the ground and flight crew of Halifax Bomber Crew 86, taken August 26, 1944. To his left is the pilot, Flight Lieutenant Bob McCullough of Port Hope, Ontario, who has just been awarded the Distinguished Flying Cross after his thirty-sixth mission. After the war, Aboussafy was a pilot as well as a fixture of the community in running Royal Bottling.

Mayfair, July, 1943

You work better refreshed

Long, hard-working hours tire you out—slow up production. You need a brief rest-pause. So, when the schedule calls for time out for a "breather," a moment for ice-cold, energy-giving "Coca-Cola" leads to better work. The delicious taste and sparkling refreshment of ice-cold "Coca-Cola" brightens any busy day.

THE COCA-COLA COMPANY OF CANADA, LIMITED

Face your refreshe

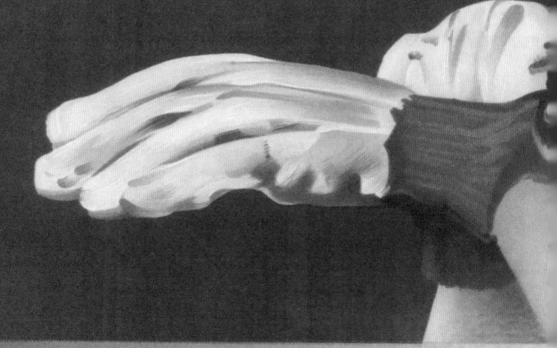

Prenez un "Coke" = Quel bon vent vous amène!

...une façon de dire aux Chinois "Fraternisons"

Dans les pays éloignés, s'il y a du Coca-Cola de disponible, c'est lui qui cimente l'amitié entre les combattants des Nations Unies. Le Coca-Cola était connu de Tientsin à Changhaï, de Hong-Kong à Tsing-Tao. Pour les Chinois comme pour les Canadiens, *Prenez un "Coke"*. sont des paroles de bienvenue, qui symbolisent la bienveillance et la liberté. De Montréal aux confins des mers, le Coca-Cola signifie *la pause qui rafraîchit*, — et est devenu le symbole des gens à l'esprit bienveillant.

* * *

Nos combattants se réjouissent de trouver du Coca-Cola dans beaucoup d'endroits outre-mer. Le Coca-Cola est un globe-trotter "de vieille date". Malgré la guerre, le Coca-Cola est aujourd'hui embouteillé sur place dans plus de 35 pays du monde — pays de l'Empire, pays alliés et pays neutres.

"Coke" = Coca-Cola
Les noms populaires acquièrent naturellement des abréviations amicales. C'est pourquoi vous entendez dire "Coke" pour Coca-Cola.

THE COCA-COLA COMPANY OF CANADA, LIMITED

(Above) Standard Coca-Cola promotional items were often translated into French for the Quebec market, which could produce unusual advertisements like this scene of American pilots enjoying a drink with Chinese soldiers.

(Opposite) A Coca-Cola ad that appeared in American newspapers on October 30, 1944.

bottom for the city of its origin. We have found them from practically every state in the Union. Just tonight I found one from Mobile, Ala. These bottles I presume came over on liners during the happier days before the war and to which we can look forward again in the future. I have been a 'Coca-Cola' fan for many years and as I said before it does take a person nearer home for a few precious minutes to sit down with a 'Coca-Cola' . . ." Corporal Short had received a letter from an old high school friend in New Jersey, who had just arrived in England with the U.S. Army. "Am looking forward to visiting him in the very near future and talking over old times with him over a bottle of 'Coca-Cola.' Hope it won' t be too long now until we can all drink our 'Coke' over the local soda fountain in our own home towns."

No one understood the importance of a seemingly small reminder of home like a bottle of Coke than the Supreme Allied Commander, General Dwight D. Eisenhower, who loved Coke and wanted his men to have as much of an opportunity to drink it as he did. In June 1943, Eisenhower sent a cable from North Africa (that was not declassified until 1966) requesting a shipment of three million bottles of Coke for the troops and ten bottling operations that could produce the same amount from syrup twice monthly, at a total capacity of twenty thousand bottles a day. Company president Robert Woodruff promised to do so at the standard price of 5 cents a bottle, regardless of what it actually cost to comply.

(Opposite) A large cardboard poster, adapted from original American artwork. (Above) A circa 1943 bilingual Victory Parade "dangler" promotion.

Prenez un "Coke" = Soyons amis

Coca-Cola

-le symbole amical

... la façon d'être bienvenu partout où vous allez

Là où la démocratie existe, vous trouvez le sentiment d'amitié, de concessions mutuelles — l'esprit de bons rapports entre voisins. Cela se compose de petites choses qui dénotent un mode de vie : sports, traitement juste, cinémas, images comiques et musique moderne. Une simple phrase comme Prenez un "Coke" fait que des étrangers deviennent des amis, et il en est de même dans les deux hémisphères. Dans le monde entier, Coca-Cola veut dire la pause qui rafraîchit — et est devenu le symbole amical des gens généreux.

THE COCA-COLA COMPANY OF CANADA, LIMITED

"Coke" = Coca-Cola
Les noms populaires acquièrent tout naturellement des abréviations amicales. C'est pourquoi vous entendez dire "Coke" pour Coca-Cola.

Things Go Better with . . . One of the world's most effective and memorable advertising campaigns was launched by Coca-Cola in 1963. But before there could be a campaign — "Things Go Better with Coke" — there had to be a product called Coke. The term had long been slang for Coca-Cola. Canadian employees in 1942 could recall hearing the term in Winnipeg in 1919 and in Toronto as early as 1913. But the company had for years discouraged the use of "Coke," as it was protective of the Coca-Cola trademark and did not want to diminish its value by introducing another term that copycat products could imitate. But in 1942 the company changed its mind and embraced the Coke label. It launched an advertising campaign, featuring the Sprite Boy character, to tell customers Coca-Cola and Coke were one and the same thing. (The company's lemon-lime soft drink, Sprite, would not appear until 1961.)

A peculiar element of the company's embrace of "Coke" was that the trademark was granted first in Canada, on July 3, 1942, and then in Newfoundland (which did not join Confederation until 1949) on November 3, 1942. The American trademark wasn't granted until 1945, although advertising had begun using Coke in 1942.

To supply Canadian and American soldiers in England, Coca-Cola relied on Harold (Bud) Smith. Born in England, Smith had emigrated to Canada in 1912 and served in the Canadian Army in the First World War. After demobilization, he joined Coca-Cola in Canada and was put in charge of production when a plant was opened in Edmonton. He then oversaw the Vancouver plant, and in 1931 returned to England to serve as plant foreman at the new bottling plant on Southfield Road in London. Smith was given the job of overseeing production of Coca-Cola for Canadian and American troops awaiting D-Day.

After D-Day, Eisenhower wanted Coca-Cola to follow on the heels of Allied troops. The company created a team of technical observers that arrived close behind the fighting and established bottling operations. One of the key technical observers was John Talley (see Chapter 3: Kelly's Team), a native of Alabama who had spent his entire ten-year Coca-Cola career in the Canadian operation. Sent overseas in September 1944, Talley accomplished the almost impossible task of getting a bottling operation going in wartime Paris soon after it was liberated. He ended up setting up the bottling plants throughout the American zone of occupation in Germany. In all, Coca-Cola established sixty-four portable bottling plants in Asia, Europe, and North Africa, and distributed more than five million bottles.

The Coca-Cola Company of Canada, Limited

HEAD OFFICE 90 BROADVIEW AVE. TORONTO

OUR NEW NAME

Coca-Cola Ltd.

November 13th, 1945

TO ALL BOTTLERS OF COCA-COLA

Our New Name - COCA-COLA LTD.

Gentlemen:

You will be interested to know that, effective November 5th, 1945, the name of our Company is changed from:

- The Coca-Cola Company of Canada, Limited, -

to

- Coca-Cola Ltd. -

Coca-Cola Ltd. is the exact official name. Please note that the last word of the name is Ltd. and not Limited.

This is merely a change of name for the purpose of achieving brevity for the convenience of our customers, our friends and our own organization. The only effect which it will have will be to necessitate the use of the new name instead of the more cumbersome old name.

The Company under the new name is fully responsible for all obligations incurred under the old name.

It is not necessary to change the name of the Company on your present stocks of such items as: crowns, bottles and cases. These should be used as required in the regular course of business. The suppliers of these items are being notified and will make the necessary changes in due course.

What's In a Name? Coca-Cola Canada relocated its headquarters from Toronto to Winnipeg in 1941, and in September 1942, president Eugene Kelly made a bold proposal to the parent firm, the Coca-Cola Company. He wanted to drop the word "Canada" from the Canadian company's name. As he explained, "This phrase stamps us in the eyes of everybody as a foreign subsidiary."

With the word "Canada" deleted, he continued, "the first step will have been taken to cause us to show up as what we are, a local company that has been operating locally for a generation." The parent company agreed, and in May 1945 the Canadian operation's name was changed to Coca-Cola, Ltd.

The
Movement
to Youth

1946–1960s

In October 1948, *The Coca-Cola Bottler*, the official publication of the Coca-Cola Company, published a remarkably long and detailed article by the Canadian Broadcasting Corporation (CBC)'s John Fisher about Canada's place in the world, especially as the Cold War took hold. Fisher recounted Canada's contributions to the last war, its economy and culture, and above all its relationship with the United States.

"For purely strategic reasons the United States should be interested in the Canadian story," Fisher concluded. "We are midway between you and the U.S.S.R. We border on three oceans. We have many riches beneath our rocks which are essential in times of emergency. Canada is a big and competent partner. We must not take our relationship for granted. We should inform each other about our problems. Because you are so big we are familiar with yours, but is not Canada to you still an unknown country? Isn't it still some place 'way up north?'"

While the wider readership of *The Coca-Cola Bottler* in the United States may have needed to better understand Canada, the company's leaders were more than aware of America's northern neighbour. As *Coca-Cola Overseas* reported in August 1948, Canada was the first place outside of the United States to bottle the beverage. There were now 125 bottlers from Vancouver to St. John's. Montreal may not have been the largest Coca-Cola plant in the world anymore, as it had become in 1934, but it was one of the top five. "Canada, always out in front, helped greatly to make Coca-Cola a year-around business beyond Labor Day, the last rose of summer, the Mason-Dixon Line," the publication saluted.

As the United States took on a new leadership role in the postwar world, Coca-Cola itself became

(Opposite) A Canadian export poster from 1950. Coca-Cola's European expansion was spearheaded out of its Canadian operations, renamed "Coca-Cola, Ltd." In 1945. (Above) A red plastic 45RMP record carrier circa 1960 with Hi-Fi Club branding.

"Lance et Compte" When the Montreal Canadiens won the 1956 Stanley Cup—the first of five straight Cup wins for the team—Coca-Cola was front and centre in the victory parade through downtown Montreal. That might have had something to do with the fact that one of its great scouts, Leo Couture, was the Coca-Cola bottler in Thetford Mines and the brother-in-law of Canadiens star Jean Béliveau (see Chapter 5: Wartime.) Every car in the parade's motorcade had a cooler stocked with Coca-Cola, and the company had the only corporate-sponsored parade float that was allowed to display its trademark. The float featured five "players," dressed in Canadiens uniforms, entertaining the crowds (both en route and in television audiences) by scoring on a Detroit goaltender. Whenever someone scored, they got to fetch a bottle of Coke from the float's cooler.

more focused on its future as a global consumer experience. Canada continued to be a model and inspiration for success in international markets, as well as a source of expertise on operating outside the United States. The efforts of Coca-Cola Export, based in New York, were entwined in the company's Canadian operations, formally renamed Coca-Cola, Ltd. in 1945 to remove the branch plant stigma. Eugene Kelly had spearheaded European expansion in the 1930s out of the Canadian operation, and operations in Cuba were managed from Canada until the Castro revolution in 1960 ended the company's bottling operations. Many key figures in the company's global expansion came through the Canadian operation (see Chapter 3: Kelly's Team).

The postwar consumer world looked nothing like the hard years of the 1930s or the sacrifices and shortages of the 1940s. There was unprecedented prosperity, a move to the suburbs by a rising middle class, a new medium called television, and a mobile culture based on the freedom of the automobile. The automobile made possible everything from shopping malls to supermarkets to drive-in movies to drive-in restaurants, which in turn were part of a new trend in fast-food or quick-service restaurants. (When McDonald's came on the scene, Coca-Cola became its beverage supplier with a handshake deal that continues today.) Prosperity brought leisure and recreation to the general public in ways and degrees not previously imagined. All these changes affected Coca-Cola—in the way it was packaged and sold, in where it was consumed, and in the variety of products that were offered to the consumer.

In the mid-1950s, Coca-Cola began to change not only what it sold but also how it was sold.

Fountain sales continued, but the drugstore soda fountain would give way to the quick-service restaurant dispenser, and bottle sales could not be restricted any longer to the standard 6.5-ounce bottle. The postwar spread of household refrigeration made possible the sale of large bottles from which individual servings could be poured. In 1955, the first "king size" bottles of Coca-Cola were introduced in the United States, and in Canada were test-marketed in Peterborough. They would become available in 10-, 12-, 16-, and 26-ounce sizes.

Packaging changes went beyond bottles, as consumers and retailers embraced cans. Steel cans had begun to proliferate in the Canadian soft drink industry in the mid-1950s. Coca-Cola, committed to the iconic shape of its glass bottle and the returnable system, resisted offering its beverages in a 12-ounce can until 1960.

Coca-Cola also diversified its product offerings. In 1955, it introduced in Naples, Italy, an orange-flavoured soda called Fanta. Such flavoured sodas had a long history with the company. Coca-Cola in Canada had bottled a line of beverages under the Gold Seal label. A Gold Seal ginger ale had been produced at the Toronto plant as early as 1908, and when the new plant and headquarters was opened in Toronto in 1923, a Gold Seal line was announced that included orangeade, cream soda, ginger ale, and "lemo-lime" flavours. Sales of Gold Seal never reached 10 per cent of bottled Coca-Cola sales in Canada in the 1930s, and by 1947 production had all but ended. But a new era of vending-machine sales demanded product variety, and Coca-Cola introduced the full Fanta line of flavoured soft drinks in 1960. The executive put in charge of Fanta was Carl M. Jernigan, who was a veteran manager with Coca-Cola in the United States when he arrived

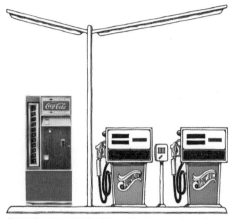

Put us where the action is.
(And we'll make you 29% happier)

apportez du Coke

EN FORMAT RÉGULIER

OU EN FORMAT ÉCONOMIQUE KING SIZE

in Canada in 1936 to head up the new fountain sales division. Jernigan stayed in Canada for twenty-five years and was assistant to the president of Coca-Cola, Ltd. when he was chosen to run Fanta.

In February 1961 came the lemon-lime Sprite, which reached the Canadian market in 1962; a diet form, Fresca, followed in 1966. TAB, the company's first diet soft drink, appeared in 1963. (Coca-Cola's experience using aspartame in TAB produced in Canada would give it the confidence to start using the artificial sweetener in Diet Coke in 1983.) Coca-Cola also diversified by acquiring the concentrated orange juice company Minute Maid in late 1960, and a plant was built in Peterborough.

Perhaps most important to Coca-Cola's role in postwar popular culture was the rise of youth culture as *the* dominant form. A baby boom—combined with prosperity, leisure, entertainment, and mass media—soon made teenagers and young adults the tastemakers. Coca-Cola, like other consumer product companies, had to learn to speak to a younger generation.

In the first years after the end of the Second World War, Coca-Cola's message to consumers associated the drink with high society and more refined entertainment. When Coca-Cola launched its radio program, "The Pause That Refreshes on the Air," in 1947, it hired an orchestra conductor and jazz arranger in Toronto, Percy Faith, who was already established as an on-air talent in Canada. By December 1950, Faith's Coca-Cola radio program was being carried on 176 stations in the CBS network in the continental United States (as well as two in Hawaii and six in Alaska), and on thirty-nine stations in Canada. Nine singers that year from Italy, Mexico, Holland, Switzerland, Argentina, France, Cuba, England, and Canada (Giselle La Fleche) were flown in to perform with Faith and his orchestra.

A baby boom soon
made teenagers
and young adults
the tastemakers.
Coca-Cola had to
learn to speak
to a younger
generation.

Coca-Cola regularly sponsored entertainment programming on CBC and had various performers under contract for promotional events. As youth culture began to take charge of popular culture in the late 1950s, Coca-Cola looked for new ways to participate. One way was Hi-Fi Club, which it launched in the United States in 1958 as a national dance program built around top-40 hits and was established in Canada by early 1959 (see the "Hi-Fi Club," page 89). Hi-Fi Club was a product of its times, a social organization run by adults for youths with the blessing of authorities such as high schools. It associated Coca-Cola with the energy of youth and pop music, but it could not last as young people in the 1960s found their own voices and embraced music as a sound-track of independence from authority. By 1962, Hi-Fi Club had come and gone, but not Coca-Cola's commitment to popular music.

Canadian pop sensation Bobby Curtola recorded for Coca-Cola "Things Go Better with Coke" in 1964, making it both a popular song and an advertising jingle.

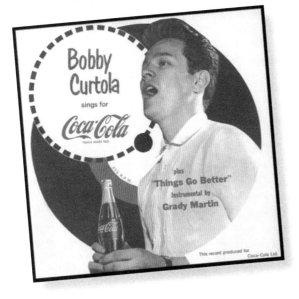

In the 1960s, Coca-Cola embraced the new sound of youth by signing a kid out of Thunder Bay, Ontario: Bobby Curtola. The Canadian teen idol had broken into the American music scene with an appearance on *The Bob Hope Show* in 1959 and had an international hit with "The Fortune Teller" in 1962. No Canadian act recorded more top-10 records in the 1960s than Curtola. In April 1964, he recorded for Coca-Cola "Things Go Better with Coke," which managed to be both a popular song and an advertising jingle. (Curtola would also record a jingle for the new slogan, "It's the Real Thing," that was introduced in 1969.) Curtola began making personal appearances for Coca-Cola and its bottlers, including autograph parties, while the company provided promotional support to his tours.

COCA-COLA LTD'S Hi-Fi CLUB

Album of Hits

DRINK Coca-Cola

Hi-Fi Club By the time teen recording sensation Bobby Curtola was helping to define a new, youthful image for Coca-Cola in Canada, the company and its bottlers were embracing the rise of pop music with a program very different from the one Canada's Percy Faith had emceed on the radio. For many teens in 1960, Coca-Cola's Hi-Fi Club was a big part of how they socialized and engaged with a form of popular music that was their own.

One of the first nationwide dance clubs in the United States, Hi-Fi Club was launched with a successful test in Indianapolis in 1958 and soon spread to Canada and Australia. In the United States, Hi-Fi Club spawned Talentsville, a national talent-search contest for high school students that offered a $5,000 scholarship or cash prize. Membership in individual clubs was open to any teenager at no cost. Events were intended to promote socially positive youth activities in association with schools and other civic groups. Dances were the most popular events, and they were hosted by a DJ who worked from a programming plan crafted by the company. Events were often broadcast by local television and radio stations. Contests were a regular feature of club promotions, and prizes included transistor radios, tie clips and bolo ties, record cases, and compilation albums. This memorabilia would become highly desirable to collectors.

Hi-Fi Club was a vibrant but short-lived phenomenon. Memorabilia gathered by Canadian Coca-Cola collector Bill Blake includes top-40 record flyers issued by Toronto radio station CHUM with Hi-Fi Club sponsorship. The earliest he has found is February 2, 1959, the last, December 18, 1961, and he believes the national club for Canada ceased operating in early 1962. Hi-Fi Club in the United States also ceased operating in the early 1960s.

DAVE JOHNSON

THE HI-FI CLUB
BROUGHT TO YOU BY
YOUR BOTTLER OF COCA-COLA
JOIN NOW!

Name

_____

Address

_____

City & Postal Zone

Mail to Hi-Fi Club, CHUM, Toronto

CHUM'S
DIAL 1050

PETE NORDHEIMER

MIKE DAROW

DAVE JOHNSON

BOB LAINE

JOHN SPRAGGE

AL BOLISKA

RIGHT CANADA 1957

HIT PARADE

Already in the United States, an array of star singing talent—including Roy Orbison, Aretha Franklin, Ray Charles, Jan and Dean, and The Coasters—had recorded versions of the "Things Go Better with Coke" song for Coca-Cola radio spots. In 1965, a Canadian version of this promotion, above and beyond Bobby Curtola's rendition, was launched. Producer Jack Richardson, then with the Toronto office of the advertising firm McCann-Erickson (which held the Coca-Cola account), enlisted recording talents that included David Clayton Thomas and the Shays, J.B. and the Playboys, and Jack London in English-language promotions. In London, Petula Clark recorded a version for the Canadian French-language market, along with Quebec artists Cesar and the Romains, Les Baronets, and Les Cailloux.

Richardson and Coca-Cola also engaged an emerging Canadian band, The Guess Who. Richardson had already worked with the Winnipeg group creating jingles, including one for Honda. In 1965, the band turned its cover of Johnny Kidd's "Shakin' All Over" (a hit for the group when it was Chad Allan and the Expressions) into a Coke radio jingle. Richardson then produced an album for Coca-Cola, *A Wild Pair*, featuring five commissioned songs from Ottawa's The Staccatos (later Five Man Electrical Band) and The Guess Who on each side. "I remember huge coolers of Coca-Cola on ice everywhere we looked in the studio," The Guess Who's Burton Cummings would recall. *A Wild Pair* was only available if you sent in ten Coca-Cola bottle cap liners and a dollar, but it sold more than enough units to have been certified as a gold record, had it been released through record stores. Several additional songs recorded during the Coca-Cola sessions by The Guess Who later appeared on their albums *Wheatfield Soul* and *Canned Wheat*.

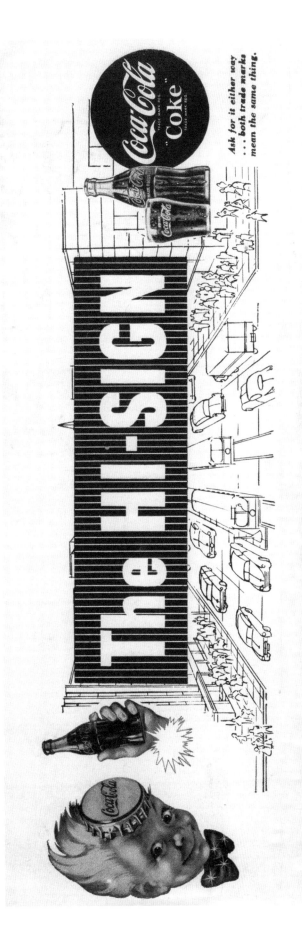

The Coca-Cola Sculpture In 1965, Coca-Cola opened a new head office and plant in Toronto, on a 13-acre site in Thorncliffe Park. The event was significant enough in the history of the company that among the attendees for the opening ceremonies was Robert Woodruff. As the new president of the Coca-Cola Company, Woodruff had recognized Coca-Cola's possibilities as a true thirst-quencher for all seasons after touring Canada in the winter of 1923–24 (see Chapter 2: Thirst Knows No Season). Eugene Kelly, so important to Coca-Cola's early success in Canada and internationally, was a guest (see Chapter 3: Kelly's Team). Also on hand was Lee Talley, who had spent the formative years of his Coca-Cola career in Canada under Kelly before becoming president in 1958 and chairman of the board in 1961. It was indeed "Old Home Week," as Coca-Cola's publication *The Refresher* remarked, and it was a testament to Canada's importance in the history of the company.

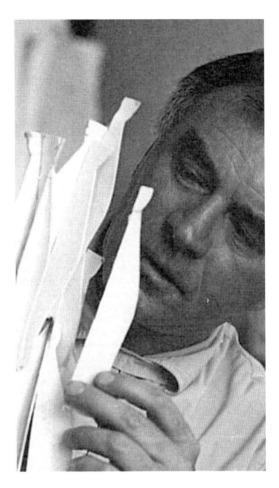

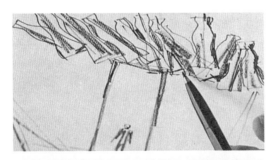

The new head office and plant inspired the company to commission a sculpture from one of Canada's leading artists, Walter Yarwood. As an abstract painter, Yarwood had been a member of Painters Eleven, but he had turned to sculpture in 1960 and fulfilled commissions for numerous major works. For the Coca-Cola commission, Yarwood took the instantly recognizable form of the Coca-Cola bottle and placed it in freeze-frame motion in 17.5 feet of bronze atop a bronze and terrazzo hemisphere.

"The sculpture demanded something dynamic and modern, a suggestion of action," Yarwood explained. "Yet it had to be an easy, everyday kind of action that would express the universal 'Pause that Refreshes' but in the youthful, vigorous idiom of today. In this way it was an unusual kind of commission, because it evolved around a consumer product, and not the sort of abstract idea that sculptors usually work with. But it was a challenging assignment for my task was to create a sculptural expression, not just about a product, but about a pleasant fact of life for millions of people."

By the mid-1960s, few consumer brands were more closely identified with youth than Coca-Cola, and it was natural that Coca-Cola should be the sponsor of the Youth Pavilion to be included as part of Expo 67 in Montreal. But Coca-Cola's frustrated efforts to make a significant contribution to the fair that marked Canada's centennial showed that the youth movement was no simple thing to address.

The pavilion was announced in February 1965 and received intense planning. As the *Montreal Gazette* explained at the time, the pavilion "will deal with the hopes and problems of modern young people and try to interpret them for adults." The associated Coca-Cola Youth Centennial Programme would give four hundred students from across the country the chance to meet at Expo 67, with all expenses paid by the company. Students entering their final year of high school in September 1967 would be eligible. They had to be honours students in every year since grade nine who also had participated and shown leadership in such extra-curricular activities as student government, athletics, drama, music, debating, public speaking, and journalism.

But by November 1965, the pavilion and youth centennial program were no more. The plan had generated endless friction about the objectives of the gathering, some of it between different regions of the country, and some critics thought it might end up being nothing more than a Hi-Fi Club dance party at a pavilion that Expo 67 organizers had sited in La Ronde, the fair's amusement park. It didn't matter that Hi-Fi Club hadn't existed for about four years. Coca-Cola realized it was facing insurmountable disagreements over the essential purpose of the pavilion and reluctantly withdrew its support, leaving it without an official presence at one of the country's milestone celebrations.

By the end of the 1960s, Coca-Cola had become synonymous with youth, a remarkable change from how it had begun the postwar era, with promotions that associated it with high society. As society overall experienced major, even tumultuous changes, Coca-Cola's relationship with youth culture shifted. It learned to be an ally of social movements rather than a manager of social activities, as Hi-Fi Club had been. And it would find ways to contribute to and advance causes, recognizing its own responsibilities on issues that were increasingly seen as global in scale.

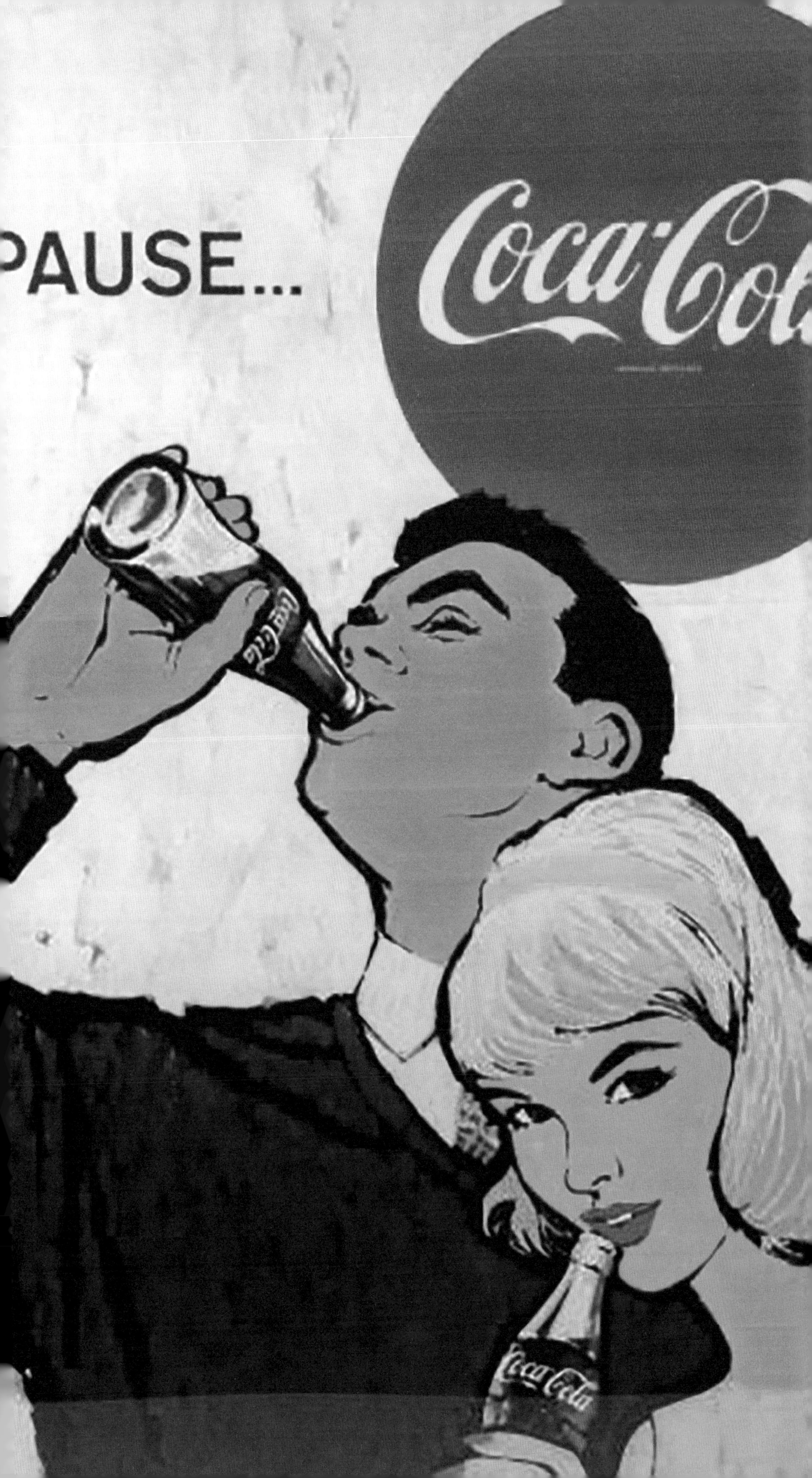
PAUSE...
Coca-Cola
Coca-Cola
Coca-Cola

"Let's Get Together/ Salut Mon Frère"

In September 1974, the organizing committee of Olympic Games Montreal 1976 announced that Coca-Cola would be the exclusive supplier of soft drinks, thus continuing the company's relationship with the Olympic Games dating back to 1928. Coca-Cola's relationship quickly grew to involve far more than beverages. Already, Coca-Cola had committed to a one-eighth sponsorship of television coverage of the Olympic Games on three Canadian networks. Coca-Cola's support of Canadian athletes, above and beyond the immediate goal of Montreal 1976, remains a high point of the company's participation in the national life of Canada. The efforts of the company and its bottlers went far beyond any typical sponsorship agreement for a major sporting event.

Canada had never before hosted an Olympic Games, and Montreal remains the only summer edition held in this country. It was an enormous undertaking not only for the city but also for the entire country, and especially for Canada's amateur athletes, who were under enormous pressure to deliver results on a home stage. Canadian amateur sport had not enjoyed strong financial support, and at Munich 1972 its athletes won just five medals (two silver and two bronze in swimming, and a bronze in sailing). Athletes were going to need all the support the country could muster for a better showing in Montreal. Coca-Cola and its bottlers accepted a leading role in raising Canada's performance and responded with energy and imagination.

Coca-Cola and its bottlers faced complex challenges simply fulfilling their duties as the official soft drink supplier. Summer Olympics include many more events and athletes, and many more venues, than Winter Olympics, and venues can be widely scattered within the country of the host city. The

Montreal, 1976 The "Youth of Canada" perform during the opening ceremonies of the twenty-first Olympiad.

Olympic Games Montreal 1976 would not help Coca-Cola introduce its beverages to Canadians. Coca-Cola would help Montreal 1976 introduce Canadians to amateur athletics.

Olympic Games, Montreal 1976 were spread over fifteen competition sites in the city alone, not to mention the Olympic Village, media facilities, and the organizing committee headquarters. Other competition sites were well beyond Montreal. Coca-Cola had to provide beverage services (some of it complimentary) to an expected twelve thousand athletes, eight thousand members of the global press, three thousand officials, and more than three million spectators. More than five hundred pieces of vending equipment were needed to dispense Coca-Cola products (Coca-Cola, Sprite, Tab, Fresca, and some Fanta flavours) just for the Montreal sites.

Outside of Montreal, company plants and franchise bottlers supplied competition sites. In Quebec, the bottler in Sherbrooke supplied two stadiums used for team handball and soccer. The Granby bottler took care of the equestrian venue at Bromont, the St-Jean bottler the shooting venue at l'Acadie, and the Joliette bottler the archery competition there. The company plant in Kingston (then a small bottling operation, with three lines producing thirty bottles a minute each, compared with the Montreal plant, with eight lines producing one hundred and fifteen to three hundred bottles a minute) shouldered the burden of supplying the sailing competition, which had six hundred competitors and trainers. Company plants in Toronto and Ottawa were called on to supply the preliminary-round soccer matches in those cities.

In the past, Coca-Cola's relationship with the Olympic movement proved to be how people in some host cities came to taste Coca-Cola for the first time. Coca-Cola was new to the Netherlands when Amsterdam hosted the Olympic Games in 1928, to Germany when the Olympic Games were held in Berlin in 1936, and to Finland

Montreal's participation medal.

when in 1952 then the Olympic Games were held in Helsinki. And while Coca-Cola was not unknown in Japan when Tokyo hosted the Olympic Games in 1964, four bottlers there had only been operating for four years. But in Montreal, there was no mystery about the taste of Coca-Cola, not with bottling having begun in the city in 1909 and its bottling operation producing more Coca-Cola than any plant in the world in 1934. Canada had continued to be a great success story for Coca-Cola, and the public's love of the product was a big advantage in assisting the country's amateur athletes, before and after 1976. Olympic Games Montreal 1976 would not help Coca-Cola introduce its beverages to Canadians. Coca-Cola would help Montreal 1976 introduce Canadians to amateur athletics.

In all, seventy Coca-Cola bottling plants and twenty-six franchised bottlers were involved in the company's commitments to the Olympic Games Montreal 1976, which were laid out in a two-year plan in 1974. A key component was encouraging the public to support the athletes' preparations for the Games. Financial assistance for athletes was critical and in short supply. Working with the Canadian Olympic Association (COA), Coca-Cola launched "Let's Get Together/Salut Mon Frère." The bottlers made an initial donation of $100,000 to the COA and made a further promise they would raise at least $100,000 from the public. Beginning in April 1975, a three-month television and radio campaign on French and English stations (which included a message from former governor-general Roland Michener) urged people to send $2 to their local Coca-Cola bottler to support the training, coaching, and equipment needs of potential Olympians. Local bottlers also arranged fundraising activities in their communities.

With Montreal 1976, Coca-Cola played a leading role in fundraising for Canada's athletes.

Coca-Cola Ltd.

ONTARIO CUP '78

INTERNATIONAL GYMNASTICS COMPETITION
NOVEMBER 14, 1978
MAPLE LEAF GARDENS
TORONTO, 8:00 P.M.

CANADA
UNITED STATES
POLAND
GERMAN DEMOCRATIC REPUBLIC
BRAZIL
UNITED KINGDOM
CZECHOSLOVAKIA
HUNGARY
U.S.S.R.
FEDERAL REPUBLIC
OF GERMANY

COUNTRIES NAMED ARE THOSE THAT HAD AGREED
TO PARTICIPATE AT TIME OF PRINTING

**Organized by The Ontario Gymnastic Federation
and supported by your local Bottler of Coca-Cola.
Presented by the Canadian Gymnastics Federation**

FOR TICKETS, CONTACT

ONTARIO CUP '78, C/O MAPLE LEAF GARDENS, 60 CARLTON STREET, TORONTO, ONTARIO M5B 1L1   TEL: (416) 368-1641

Coca-Cola is a registered trade mark which identifies only the product of Coca-Cola Ltd.

Enjoy *Coca-Cola*

Meanwhile, Coca-Cola in Canada pursued two major events to raise funds for Olympians, above and beyond those competing in Montreal 1976. The first was Real Thing on Ice, a benefit figure skating revue featuring Winter Olympic Games hopefuls as Innsbruck 1976 approached. The performers included Toller Cranston, who would win bronze in Innsbruck, one of only three Canadian medals at those Olympic Games. Held before a sellout crowd at Maple Leaf Gardens in September 1975, proceeds were divided between "Let's Get Together/Salut Mon Frère"

and the Canadian Figure Skating Association. The event became a prime-time CBC special on Christmas Day. Watched by one-quarter of Canadian households, it greatly boosted fundraising awareness. The second Coca-Cola initiative was a nation-wide series of Olympathon fundraising walks held in conjunction with Lions International and local bottlers. The "Let's Get Together/Salut Mon Frère" campaign wildly exceeded expectations, raising $350,000, which Coca-Cola and its bottlers turned over to the COA.

Coca-Cola also made one of the most unusual gestures of support for an Olympic team. The company extended its established relationship with equestrian sport by buying a horse, Regardez, and donating it to the Canadian equestrian team for training and competition. While Regardez was not a mount at Montreal 1976, team captain Jim Elder did compete aboard him in subsequent events. As it happened, equestrian was one of the events in which Canada did bring home a medal in 1976, a silver for Michel Vaillancourt. In all, Canada won eleven medals in 1976 (five silver, six bronze), an improvement over Munich that made Canadians realize still greater things were possible if Canadian athletes received better, longer-term support.

The Montreal experience was so positive that Coca-Cola became the official soft drink supplier of the 1978 Commonwealth Games in Edmonton. The company also struck a four-year agreement with the COA to be the official soft drink supplier to the Canadian Olympic team. As part of the agreement, Coca-Cola would raise funds for the COA and help individual sports federations by sponsoring athletic events and lending business expertise and guidance. It was the beginning of a surge in Canadian pride in its amateur athletes and of world-class performances in a wide variety of athletic disciplines.

(Above) Coca-Cola's experience supporting Montreal 1976 was so positive it became the official soft drink supplier of the 1978 Commonwealth Games in Edmonton. (Opposite) One of the most unusual Olympic sponsorships in history was Coca-Cola's donation of a horse, Regardez, to the Canadian equestrian team, shown here with team captain Jim Elder.

The
Community
Bottler

Look inside the display case of the Midland Bay Sailing Club and you will find the Penetang Bottling Co. Trophy. Donated in 1971 by the Coca-Cola bottler in the neighbouring harbour town of Penetanguishene, Ontario, on southeastern Georgian Bay, it is awarded to the community club's dinghy racing champion every season.

Butch Orser, who at the time of the sailing trophy donation was managing the bottling company and in the process of acquiring majority ownership, spent some time in the navy, but he was not a recreational sailor. "Like any business in a community, you would be asked for sponsorship of everything and anything," says Janice Thompson, one of Butch Orser's two daughters, who would come to serve as his officer manager while her husband managed the bottling plant. "A school would approach us and say, 'We need one hundred dollars for an award for a top student,' and we just did it."

Coca-Cola bottlers like Penetang Bottling Co. were family-run fixtures of small communities. From the beginning of the company's bottling history in Canada in 1906, until changes in the soft drink industry overall led Coca-Cola to reacquire its bottling franchises in the late 1980s (see "The Change in Bottling," page 120), these bottlers were a big part of how Canadians got to know Coca-Cola and of how Coca-Cola built its relationship with retailers, consumers, and communities. The story of the Penetang Bottling Co. is emblematic of bottler stories across the country.

Penetang Bottling Co. was founded in 1917 by Abe Moses, the son of a Russian immigrant, Max. Abe was a local farmer who made a switch to the hotel and tavern business. Around 1907, Abe and a brother bought a downtown Penetanguishene fixture, the Georgian Bay Hotel, and Abe became

Coca-Cola bottlers were family-run fixtures of small communities.

(Above) Local bottling companies thrived in provinces throughout Canada, including the Regina, Saskatchewan plant that celebrated 60 years of bottling in their community in 1981, marked by this commemorative tray from the Coca-Cola archives.

Butch Orser of Penetang Bottling Co. was the quintessential small-town Coca-Cola bottler.

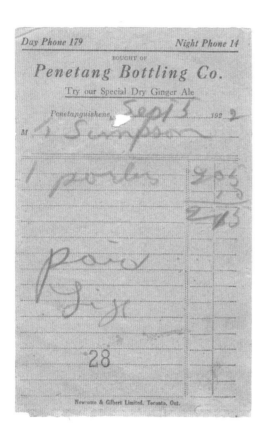

An 1922 order form for Penetang Bottling Co.

sole proprietor in 1910. His first wife, Annie, had died in 1909, and in December 1910, Abe remarried, to Mary Lucy (Minnie) Dubeau, who had a daughter, Hellen, from a previous marriage. A daughter born to Abe and Minnie, Margaret, followed in 1911. In 1917, Abe branched into soft drinks, founding the bottling company, which he moved into the hotel basement in 1919. Penetang Bottling made soda water and a variety of flavoured drinks, including Whistle Orange and a ginger ale sold under names like Georgian Bay Dry and Dominion Dry.

The Georgian Bay Hotel was destroyed in a catastrophic fire in 1921 and was never rebuilt. Abe Moses got the bottling works going again on a new property across the street, and it was probably in the course of resuming business that he became a franchise Coca-Cola bottler. In the late 1930s, Coca-Cola suspended its bottling licence for Orillia, Ontario, about 30 miles east of Penetanguishene, and an expansion of Penetang Bottling documented in a photo in May 1941 probably was due to the Orillia territory being awarded to Moses.

Abe Moses died in 1947, and the bottling business passed to his two daughters. Margaret's husband, Ted Cuthbert, was involved as manager, but community members agree that Hellen Booth, Abe Moses's stepdaughter, was very much in charge. "Hellen Booth had a cottage out our way on Sawlog Bay," local resident Bill Mackie recalls. "She called it 'coka-cabana' or something. Back in the day—as a kid—I thought she owned the entire company, and all the products for the entire world were made at the Penetanguishene plant."

Under Hellen Booth's direction, the bottling works underwent a major expansion in 1956 in a new location on Main Street in Penetanguishene. Daniel A. Dubeau can remember working for his great-aunt as a summer job; his father had been employed at the bottler when Abe Moses owned it in the 1930s. "I worked on the production line, watching clean bottles passing a blue light for two hours, then packing the full bottles into wood cases for two hours, then rotating again. Payday was every Friday. At my level I could take a six-pack of any product."

Meanwhile, Butch Orser was just getting started on a career with Coca-Cola, after a spell in the Royal Canadian Navy aboard the aircraft carrier HMCS *Magnificent*. Around 1955, he began working as a salesman for Coca-Cola in Windsor, Ontario, driving a truck to service accounts such as corner stores. In 1961, he transferred to Belleville, Ontario, and in 1965 he came to Penetanguishene to strike a deal with Hellen Booth that benefited both of them. For $10,000, Butch bought 10 per cent of Penetang Bottling. The agreement specified that as Butch improved sales, he would acquire an ever-greater share of the company. The arrangement provided security to Hellen, who was about to turn sixty, and

Company trucks deliver Coca-Cola in the 1920s.

Community involvement meant Penetang Bottling had to have a parade float. "Like any business in a community, you would be asked for sponsorship of everything and anything," Jane Thompson, one of Butch Orser's two daughters, remembers.

an incentive to Butch to make the business grow. After fourteen years, in 1979, Penetang Bottling belonged entirely to Butch Orser. He also expanded through a partnership with Bob Marshall in Highland Beverages, which was the Coca-Cola franchise bottler in Uxbridge and Peterborough, Ontario.

Under Butch Orser, Penetang Bottling was a classic family enterprise that involved to varying degrees all five of his children. His son Michael recalls working in all aspects of the operation: the production line, the warehouse, sorting returned bottles. Janice as noted ran the office and looked after finances. MaryKay (Melnyk) and Brian as kids were busy with figure skating. MaryKay would skate professionally, and from 1981 to 1987 Brian won eight straight national men's singles titles. He also won the 1987 world title, silver medals at the 1984 and 1988 Olympic Games, and carried the flag for the Canadian team in the 1988 opening ceremonies in Calgary. Still, while Saturday might have been for skating practice, MaryKay can remember going

Partners **Bob Marshall (left) and Butch Orser.**

choose it

The same great taste of Coca-Cola.
In convenient one-way bottles, or
low cost returnables.
Take your pick.
Things go better with
the taste of Coke.

to the bottling operation after church on Sunday to fix labels on bottles, before her dad invested in a mechanized labeller.

"Coca-Cola was good at taking care of their bottlers," says MaryKay. Franchise bottlers such as Penetang Bottling Co. did more than bottle—they had distribution rights for Coca-Cola's products. In addition to bottling various Coca-Cola beverages, including Sprite and Fanta, the Orsers also bottled A&W root beer and Schweppes ginger ale through the licences held by Coca-Cola ("I even had a dog named Schweppes," MaryKay says), and as a distributor handled the Coca-Cola products that were sold in cans. Coca-Cola also listened to Butch Orser. "My father had a lot of ingenuity, and the company was quite open to the ideas he came up with."

Penetang Bottling became its own extended family for employees. "People that worked for us usually worked for us their whole life," says MaryKay. Whether the jobs were in franchise bottling operations such as

A Family Business In his youth (when he wasn't training to become a figure skating world champion and two-time Olympian), Brian Orser, together with his siblings, worked for their father at the bottling plant in Penatanguishene, Ontario.

People that worked for us usually worked for us their whole life.

MaryKay (Orser) Melnyk

Penetang Bottling or in plants owned by Coca-Cola, they offered careers with good wages and benefits to people who often had a high school education or less and gave them the chance to move up. Butch Orser "understood the philosophy that if you surround yourself with good people, you will be rewarded," says Michael.

"He was a very dedicated bottler," says Janice, "very loyal to his customers." A local store might only want five cases of a product when Coca-Cola's policy was to fulfill minimum orders of ten cases, but Butch will fill it anyway. He also serviced soft drink vending machines, and if a customer needed help on a Saturday, he was there. "He instilled that dedication in the staff, and in the family," says Janice.

Butch Orser might have been a franchisee, but he was every inch a "Coke" man. When the company celebrated its one-hundredth anniversary in 1986, Janice remembers, "My father felt it extremely important for all of his key people to attend the celebrations. He wanted everyone to understand the history of the company." The entire upper management at Penetang Bottling and Highland Beverages, along with their spouses, were taken to Atlanta at Butch Orser's and Bob Marshall's expense. When Brian competed at Calgary 1988 the family tacked on a ski holiday outfitted in matching Coca-Cola ski suits that Butch ordered from the company's available promotional items.

It was around this time that the era

For Penetang Bottling, Coca-Cola bound together family, community life, and friends.

The Change in Bottling In 1986, Coca-Cola in the United States created Coca-Cola Enterprises, Inc., to which it transferred most of the company's American bottling operations, and went public with an offering of 51 per cent of its stock. In 1987, Coca-Cola made a similar change in Canada. In July 1987, a new company, T.C.C. Bottling Ltd., was formed, which would be owned 49 per cent by Coca-Cola, Ltd., the Canadian branch of Coca-Cola, and 51 per cent by public shareholders. T.C.C. Bottling would also own Canada Dry Bottling Company Ltd., which held the licence for Canada Dry soft drinks in Alberta and Ontario. At the same time, T.C.C. Bottling was acquiring the franchise bottling rights of the many independent bottlers across the country. (T.C.C. Bottling's name would be changed to Coca-Cola Beverages in 1989.) When the new bottling structure was announced, Coca-Cola's own bottling plants produced about 55 per cent of the company's sales. By 1991, as franchise bottlers were absorbed, Coca-Cola Beverages accounted for 93 per cent of sales in Canada and was the fourth-largest Coca-Cola bottler in the world, with nineteen plants and sixty-two distribution centres. Today, all Coca-Cola products are bottled in Canada by Coca-Cola Beverages.

of the franchise bottler ended, as Coca-Cola in Canada restructured. Highland Beverages was sold to Coca-Cola in 1987, while Penetang Bottling continued until 1989, with the Orsers retaining the real estate they owned. As MaryKay recalls, although the bottling and distribution operation in Penetanguishene was closed as a result, all of the employees were guaranteed employment by Coca-Cola.

Today, mentioning Penetang Bottling, Abe Moses, the Booth sisters, and the Orsers immediately triggers waves of nostalgia among long-time local residents. They remember the full-time and summer jobs, the parade floats, the small fortunes kids amassed collecting bottles and returning them, the soft drink cans one employee would hand out every Halloween that made his house the first and the last stop of every trick-or-treat. And then there is the dinghy trophy on display in the community sailing club, quietly reminding everyone of the constant contributions Butch Orser made to the local community.

Spectacle and Society

When Calgary was awarded the 1988 Winter Olympic Games in 1981, only five years had passed since Montreal 1976. Calgary had seven years to prepare for its Games, the first Winter Olympics to be hosted by a major metropolitan city. Coca-Cola would mark its diamond anniversary of association with the Olympics. Sixty years had passed since Coca-Cola had shipped one thousand cases of its beverage to the Olympic Games Amsterdam 1928 to refresh the American team. Forty-six countries had participated (including female athletes, for the first time, in track and field). Calgary would see sixty-four nations send athletes, a record for a Winter Olympics.

Twenty-two years later, the Winter Olympic Games would be back in Canada, in Vancouver. Coca-Cola was again at the forefront of the celebrations. The Olympics returned to a country that embraced the Games as an opportunity not only to win medals and host a global celebration of sport but also to mount a global spectacle that adhered to values shared by Canadians with the world at large. As a sponsor, Coca-Cola was committed to ensuring its own performance delivered on those values. As it happened, Coca-Cola had already embarked on its own initiatives in social and environmental responsibility that dovetailed well with the challenges and opportunities of Vancouver 2010.

Olympic sponsorship had changed significantly since 1976, when the Olympic Games returned to Canada in 1988. Where Coca-Cola had been the official soft drink supplier to the Montreal Games through an arrangement with the host organizing committee, sponsorship in 1988 had moved to a global level with the International Olympic Committee (IOC). As a result, Coca-Cola was a worldwide sponsor of both

(Above) To commemorate the Olympics Games Vancouver 2010, Coca-Cola produced a set of trading pins—one pin for each day of the games. Placed together they form a Coca-Cola contour bottle. (Opposite) A photo detailing the 'Nawala' Coke bottle by artist Calvin Hunt, created as part of the Coca-Cola Aboriginal Art Bottle Program for the Vancouver 2010 Olympics.

Calgary 1988 and the Summer Olympics to follow in Seoul, South Korea. Coca-Cola's Canadian operations were on the front lines of fulfilling the company's duties in Calgary, but the global Coca-Cola family was involved to some degree.

There had also been an important change in how Coca-Cola was organized in Canada since the Montreal Games, and it happened almost on the eve of the Calgary Games. Beginning in July 1987, the Coca-Cola bottling system was completely transformed with the creation of T.C.C. Bottling and the acquisition of the contracts of franchise bottlers (see page 120, "The Change in Bottling"). And so it happened that the weight of fulfilling Coca-Cola's obligations as the official soft drink supplier in Calgary fell on a new enterprise, the Calgary branch of T.C.C. Bottling, with a big assist from the rest of Coca-Cola in Canada.

Diamond Anniversary In Calgary, Coca-Cola celebrated sixty years with the Olympic Games.

Soft drinks had to be provided not only to the many spectators but also to ten thousand volunteers at all Olympic venues, five thousand members of the international media, and twenty-five hundred athletes, as well as dignitaries and other sponsors. Each site had a 45-foot trailer, where product was delivered daily from midnight to 6 a.m. In all, about 475 pieces of equipment had to be installed at sites. Coca-Cola also created Lift, an energy drink for the athletes.

To mark its diamond jubilee with the Olympic Games, Coca-Cola made two innovative contributions to Calgary 1988. One was the Coca-Cola Olympic Pin Trading Centre in downtown Calgary (see "The Other Sport at Calgary 1988," page 125). The other was the Coca-Cola World Chorus, which performed before an estimated global audience of 2.2. billion at the opening ceremonies, as well as at the closing ceremonies. Their song, "Can't You Feel It?" was commissioned by the Calgary Olympic Organizing Committee and Coca-Cola from the multiple Grammy-winning Canadian composer/producer David Foster, with lyrics by Foster and Tommy Banks, the musical director of the opening and closing ceremonies. The composition of the forty-two-strong choir, young men and women age eighteen to twenty-five, was the subject of a global talent search. Twenty-three nations held selections organized by the local Coca-Cola bottling operation, and each nation found its own way to make their choices. An estimated three hundred million people in China watched a televised selection of two students from the Central Music Conservatory in Beijing. New Zealand's choice was a young woman whose mother sang at the Olympic Games in Melbourne in 1956. In Canada, commercials on CTV encouraged viewers to call a toll-free number and submit an audiotape as well as an essay. Twelve finalists were chosen for an audition in Toronto, from which the Canadian contingent of the choir was selected.

When the Winter Olympics returned to Canada in February 2010 in Vancouver, Coca-Cola again was at the forefront of the celebrations, not only as the official beverage supplier but also as a co-presenter with Royal Bank of Canada (RBC) of the Olympic and Paralympic Torch Relays. The Torch Relay for Calgary had been the longest one ever, covering some 18,000 kilometres over eighty-eight days, with the contest for torch-bearer selection generating six million entries. For Vancouver, the Torch Relay was even larger—about one hundred days, with twelve thousand torch-bearers carrying the Olympic flame through about one thousand participating communities.

The Other Sport at Calgary 1988 Pin trading had become popular with spectators at Lake Placid 1980 and Los Angeles 1984. It became an unofficial Olympic sport at Calgary 1988 through the Coca-Cola Olympic Pin Trading Centre. Calgary's Olympic Organizing Committee commissioned about six hundred new Olympic pin designs for the Games, including nearly ninety provided by Coca-Cola and its worldwide bottler system. In all, more than seven million pins were produced for Calgary during the two years leading up to the Games. Coca-Cola also published a guide to Olympic pin trading, and a free symposium on "The Art of Pin Trading" was even held at the University of Calgary, co-sponsored by the University of Calgary Students Union. For three hours, seven experts debated the trading phenomenon. So popular was pin trading that a collectors club with 160 members sprang up in Calgary.

The Coca-Cola Olympic Pin Trading Centre was located in downtown Calgary, in the Coca-Cola/Calgary International Plaza, a joint project of the company and the city. Other sponsors included the Calgary Canadian Citizenship Council and the Calgary Folk Arts Council. The plaza featured several large-screen monitors to provide televised coverage of competition, the Canada Safeway Ltd. Food Fair (featuring twenty kiosks of ethnic cuisine), and the Northern Telecom Entertainment Stage.

Collecting Coca-Cola Few companies have created a body of memorabilia as deep and as wide—and as tempting to collectors—as Coca-Cola. From the earliest days under the Candler family, Coca-Cola was renowned for its imaginative use of a wide variety of distinctive signage and promotional items. Other practical items, such as coolers and fountain dispensers, greatly increased the amount of potential memorabilia. And then of course there are the bottles: many, many bottles, in different shapes and of different origins. At the same time, the icons of the brand—the script logo and the contour bottle—have made Coca-Cola materials timeless in their recognition and appeal.

Collecting Coca-Cola memorabilia seems to have caught fire in the early 1970s. The pastime became formally organized in January 1975, with the founding of The Coca-Cola Clan, now known as The Coca-Cola Collectors Club. Sixty of its 185 members converged on Atlanta that August for their first annual gathering of what truly became a clan of enthusiasts, with more than forty chapters now operating worldwide, including one in Ontario as well as a national one for Canada.

The club's president and founder, Bob Buffaloe, a schoolteacher in Memphis, Tennessee, had only begun collecting company memorabilia three years earlier. "My wife and I have both become avid collectors of memorabilia for Coke," he explained after the first gathering. "It occupies every weekend. Our entire free time revolves around collecting. . . . You've never seen a more enthusiastic group of people than collectors of items advertising Coke because such materials are so depictive of the history and mood of America at various times in our history."

The bug of collecting Coca-Cola bit hard in Canada at the same as it did in the United States. Canadians were among the founding members of The Coca-Cola Clan in 1975. With Coca-Cola having enjoyed a history almost as long in Canada as in the United States, there was a tremendous variety of material waiting to be found, and sometimes literally dug up, and Canada offered its own unique items to discerning collectors.

Bill Cook (above at a yard sale in Brampton, Ontario) has been collecting since the late 1970s. As president of the Ontario chapter of the Coca-Cola Collectors Club, his basement (opposite) is a shrine to his enthusiasm.

Ron Antonio, president of the Canadian chapter of Coca-Cola Collectors, got started around 1973, when was he was about twenty-two years old, after being given a Coke machine for Christmas. "I thought, 'I'll get a sign to go with it.'" There was no turning back. A few years later, his father got into collecting, and it was a visit to Ron's father in 1978 that helped launch Bill Cook on his Coca-Cola passion. Bill was collecting pop bottles, and he traded some to Ron's father for a "door bar," a kind of Coca-Cola sign that went at the top of the door, as well as another sign. He is now president of the Ontario chapter of Coca-Cola Collectors and has a basement shrine to Coca-Cola memorabilia that is a treasure-trove of the company's Canadian history and its place in popular culture.

Coca-Cola memorabilia spans so many collecting categories that enthusiasts can easily specialize, whether the category is sports, bottles, signage, coolers, advertising—you name it. Bill Blake is one such Canadian collector, who specializes in the music side while still collecting a variety of Coca-Cola material. He got his start collecting Coca-Cola in the mid-1980s. "I always liked antiques and old stuff. In high school my girlfriend, now my wife, and I started collected pieces, and then we focused on Coke." He realized how big the Coca-Cola collecting hobby was when he took an item to an antique dealer while on vacation in Florida. "I asked him, 'What do you think it's worth?' He said, 'Let's look it up in the book.' And I thought, 'There's a book?' You think you are the only person collecting Coca-Cola, and then you find out there's a club."

Clearly, it is the social aspect of collecting that has drawn so many people to Coca-Cola memorabilia, and has kept them there. "I look at it as the Coca-Cola family," says Bill Cook. "It's the friendships you make over the years. It's not the same if you just buy things on eBay."

Lisa Shepherd/Métis

**Elliot Doxtater/
Ontario First Nations**

Phyllis Grant/Mi'kmaq

Its 35,000-kilometre route covered the greatest distance within a single country of any Torch Relay. A typical day saw the Olympic torch carried 250 kilometres for six hours, with each relay participant bearing it for about 200 metres. Another four hours of programming were held at each participating community.

Coca-Cola added a unique element to the relay by organizing an exhibition of original works by Indigenous artists. The Vancouver Games were co-hosted by four First Nations (Lil'wat, Musqueam, Squamish, and Tsleil-Waututh), and the art program met a goal of the Vancouver Olympic Committee (VANOC) to achieve an unprecedented level of Indigenous participation. Working with VANOC, Coca-Cola invited Indigenous artists to apply for the opportunity to create an original statement about their culture, employing the shape of a Coca-Cola bottle. Fifty-three artists reached a final round of proposals adjudicated by six experts in Indigenous art, with ten chosen to create their visions. The artists' costs were covered and an honorarium paid, and all of the completed works were auctioned to support a 2010 Aboriginal Youth Legacy Fund. During the Torch Relay, the art bottles, which ranged from 4 to 6 feet in height and were executed in fibreglass or wood, were displayed in a travelling exhibit in relay host communities, delivering unprecedented exposure to the work of individual artists and the messages the striking bottles delivered. During the Games, all the artists' efforts were on display at various sites in Vancouver.

Tanya Mesher/Inuit

Christy Groves/Métis

**Corrine Hunt
Kwakiutl/Tlingit**

Lionel Peyachew/Plains Cree

Kim Stewart/Métis

**Calvin Hunt/
B.C. First Nations**

Dawn Oman/Métis

Alan Syliboy/Mi'kmaq

**Alaynee Goodwill
Dakota/Lakota**

**Garry Oker/
B.C. First Nations**

Jerry Ell/Inuit

Jackie Traverse/Anishinabe

Coca-Cola also sponsored the Torch Relay for the 2010 Paralympic Games, held in Vancouver in March 2010, continuing an association it had begun with the Paralympics in Barcelona in 1992. Thirteen Canadian communities were visited by the torch over a ten-day relay.

Sustainability was one of the key values VANOC identified in its planning for the 2010 Olympics, and as the official beverage supplier, Coca-Cola responded with an array of commitments and initiatives that earned it a Sustainability Star from VANOC for its carbon footprint and offset program. Coca-Cola's sustainability plan for the Vancouver Games was developed through consultation with World Wildlife Fund-Canada and the David Suzuki Foundation. Coca-Cola committed to a carbon-neutral perform- ance in its sponsorship of the Olympic Games and the Torch Relay. All of the cups and lids used for products were compostable, and its new PlantBottle, made from up to 30 per cent plant fibre, was used for most Coca-Cola products. Coca-Cola also committed to diverting at least 95 per cent of waste generated by its products sold at Games venues from landfills. Coca-Cola recycled its own concentrate barrels into more than eight hundred recycling barrels to collect beverage containers. Concessions were constructed with post-consumer recycled plastic. All Coca-Cola associ- ates at the Games wore uniforms made from recycled plastic bottles. At three official Pin Trading Centres hosted by Coca-Cola, visitors could trade more than 130 different Vancouver 2010 lapel pins that were made from recycled material.

Sustainability Star. Coca-Cola was a win-
ner with its carbon-neutral performance.

The Sogo Carry the Flame Tour launched a five-year effort to increase physical activity in Canadian youth. By 2015, Coca-Cola Canada was committed to a $10 million investment.

The Olympic Winter Games Vancouver 2010 was a showcase as well as a test of Coca-Cola's global corporate initiatives to reduce its own impact on the planet and improve the quality of life for individuals, families, and communities. The Live Positively initiative, which promotes active and healthy lifestyles, experienced its third Olympic Games. During the Games, Live Positively Awards were made to individuals and organizations that make positive choices and strive to better themselves, their communities, and others in their everyday lives. The Sogo Carry the Flame Tour was a highly visible launch to an initial five-year Canadian commitment to Sogo Active, mounted by Coca-Cola Canada and ParticipACTION to increase physical activity in Canadian youth. The tour visited twenty-seven communities across the country to promote active living for youth and encourage participation in the coming Torch Relay. In all, Coca-Cola Canada by 2015 was committed to a $10 million investment over ten years to help teens be active. By then, about four hundred thousand Canadian youths in more than five thousand communities had been engaged through the ParticipACTION Teen Challenge. Other active-living support has benefited Boys and Girls Clubs of Canada, the Breakfast Club of Canada, and the Abilities Centre for adults with disabilities.

(Above) Olympic torches from previous Games on display at the Sogo Carry the Flame tour. (Opposite) The PlantBottle is made with up to 30 per cent plant-based material, reducing its carbon impact. And it is 100 per cent recyclable.

The company's sustainability commitments extended to its Post-Olympic Games Legacy Project, as Coca-Cola Canada made a $350,000 investment in inner-city Vancouver youth. The Coca-Cola Inner City Sport Court in the Ray-Cam community features a playing surface made from recycled plastic bottles. In addition to funding commitments to Ray-Cam Cooperative Community Centre for programming, coaching, and a variety of sports clinics, Coca-Cola donated seven thousand toques, scarves, and vests made from recycled containers gathered during the Games.

In addition to the first major usage of PlantBottle, Vancouver 2010 marked the North American debut of a new refrigerant technology. Some fourteen hundred proprietary EKOfresh refrigeration units were deployed by Coca-Cola, which nearly eliminate direct greenhouse gas emissions and reduce energy use by 35 per cent over regular refrigeration units through "smart" temperature control. Their reduction of 5,600 metric tonnes of emissions was the equivalent of taking about twelve hundred cars off the road for an entire year. It was an impressive start to the company's commitment to eliminate the use of hydrofluorocarbon gases in its vending machines worldwide. These and other initiatives were part of Coca-Cola's 2020 Vision for meeting an array of sustainability goals in its operations, which include the "5 by 20" initiative that hopes to empower five million women entrepreneurs by 2020. Coca-Cola had also committed to increasing the number of women in system leadership roles within the company. "Women" represent one of the three Ws in Coca-Cola's sustainability and Live Positively goals, the other two being "waste" and "water."

The company's sustainability commitments included a new refrigeration technology which reduced energy use by 35%—the equivalent of taking twelve hundred cars off the road for a year.

A Long-Standing Friendship In 2012, Coca-Cola Canada
used footage from the IMAX film *To the Arctic 3D* as
part of their efforts to help preserve polar bear habitat
in Canada's north. It was not the first time the company
and the iconic animals had partnered up, as seen in this
1922 poster from France.

Preserving an Arctic Home Coca-Cola's association with winter dates back to the "Thirst Knows No Season" slogan of 1921 and produced the iconic jolly Santa Claus created for Coca-Cola promotions by artist Haddon Sundblom in 1931. Hockey was also a natural winter fit, and NHL star Wayne Gretzky served as a company spokesperson. In 1993, Coca-Cola's winter-themed imagery received a phenomenally popular update with the debut of the animated polar bear family.

In 2011, Coca-Cola's iconic association with polar bears led to a major partnership with World Wildlife Fund (WWF). "Arctic Home" was launched to raise awareness of climate change and help preserve the northern habitats of these bears, which covers as much as 500,000 square miles, as well as protect the cultural and economic needs of people living in this northern landscape.

Coca-Cola had already made donations of more than $1 million over the previous four years to WWF's arctic research and conservation efforts. For the new "Arctic Home" program, Coca-Cola made an initial donation pledge of $2 million over five years to WWF. The company then launched a public awareness campaign that invited the public to contribute as well, with a commitment to WWF to raise at least an additional $1 million. From November 2011 to February 2012, Coca-Cola beverages were sold in limited-edition white cans featuring a mother polar bear and two cubs crossing an arctic landscape. Bottled products featured a special white bottle cap. By texting a code from these special-edition packages, consumers could donate a dollar to WWF's conservation work in polar bear habitat.

It was the only time the iconic colours of Coca-Cola's red-and-white cans had been changed in Canada, other than special-edition packaging for the Winter Olympic Games Vancouver 2010. "Branding is connected to colour and to walk away from your primary colour is an important step," Coca-Cola Canada president Nicola Kettlitz told Canadian Press. "It makes a very big statement of support."

Coca-Cola also struck a partnership with MacGillivray Freeman Films, co-producers of a new IMAX film, *To the Arctic 3D*. Scheduled for release in 2012, the film followed a mother polar bear and two cubs through the arctic environment. Footage from the coming film was featured in Coca-Cola's "Arctic Home" television promotions, and the fundraising campaign's website provided preview footage.

As WWF-Canada CEO Gerald Butts explained to Canadian Press, "What we're after is looking at all of the change that's going to take place in the Arctic over the next 25 to 60 years and getting ahead of it by predicting where the last permanent sea ice is likely to persist and protect that area, not just for polar bears but for every ice-dependent species in the Arctic."

GRAB A *Coca-Cola*.
MAKE A DIFFERENCE.

PURCHASE SPECIALLY MARKED **12-CAN PACKAGES**†
AND COCA-COLA® WILL DONATE 5% OF THE PROCEEDS
TO WWF-CANADA TO HELP PROTECT THE
POLAR BEARS' ARCTIC HOME·

EVERY ACTION MATTERS, FIND OUT HOW ELSE
YOU CAN PLEDGE YOUR SUPPORT AT
www.livepositively.ca/arctichome

Water has been one of the greatest focal points. Coca-Cola entered into a global partnership with World Wildlife Fund in 2007 aimed at water conservation. In Canada alone since 2008, Coca-Cola had donated more than six thousand concentrate barrels to be used as rain barrels. Donations of $1 million have helped WWF-Canada preserve and protect watersheds. A $500,000 contribution to a Toronto water restoration project is expected to reduce contamination to more than 1 million cubic metres of water per year. Globally, Coca-Cola estimated a reduction in its own water usage of 1 billion litres and aims to achieve a system-wide improvement in water usage of 25 per cent by 2020. Perhaps Coca-Cola's best known environmental initiative has been Arctic Home, in which a partnership with WWF raised by 2015 more than $5 million to protect the arctic habitat of polar bears (see "Preserving an Arctic Home," page 137).

When Coca-Cola began dispensing from soda-fountain taps in Canada in 1897, no one would have imagined that its future in Canada would include saving the habitat of polar bears threatened by climate change. Canadian winters had convinced Coca-Cola that thirst truly knew no season, and its success in Canada helped it become a global enterprise, operating in more countries than there are members of the United Nations. The refreshment that was a reminder of home to soldiers in the Second World War was now at home around the planet. And as Coca-Cola got bigger, the world got smaller, with its challenges and hopes shared by all.

The idea of "sharing" has been part of Coca-Cola's message since at least 1915. "Share a Coke with someone," one advertisement suggested in 1969. "Coca-Cola seems to bring more people together than anything else in the world." A polar bear and two cubs struggling to survive in the Canadian arctic became important to the world at large, a shared responsibility. Thirst knows no season, and the challenges of society and the environment know no borders.

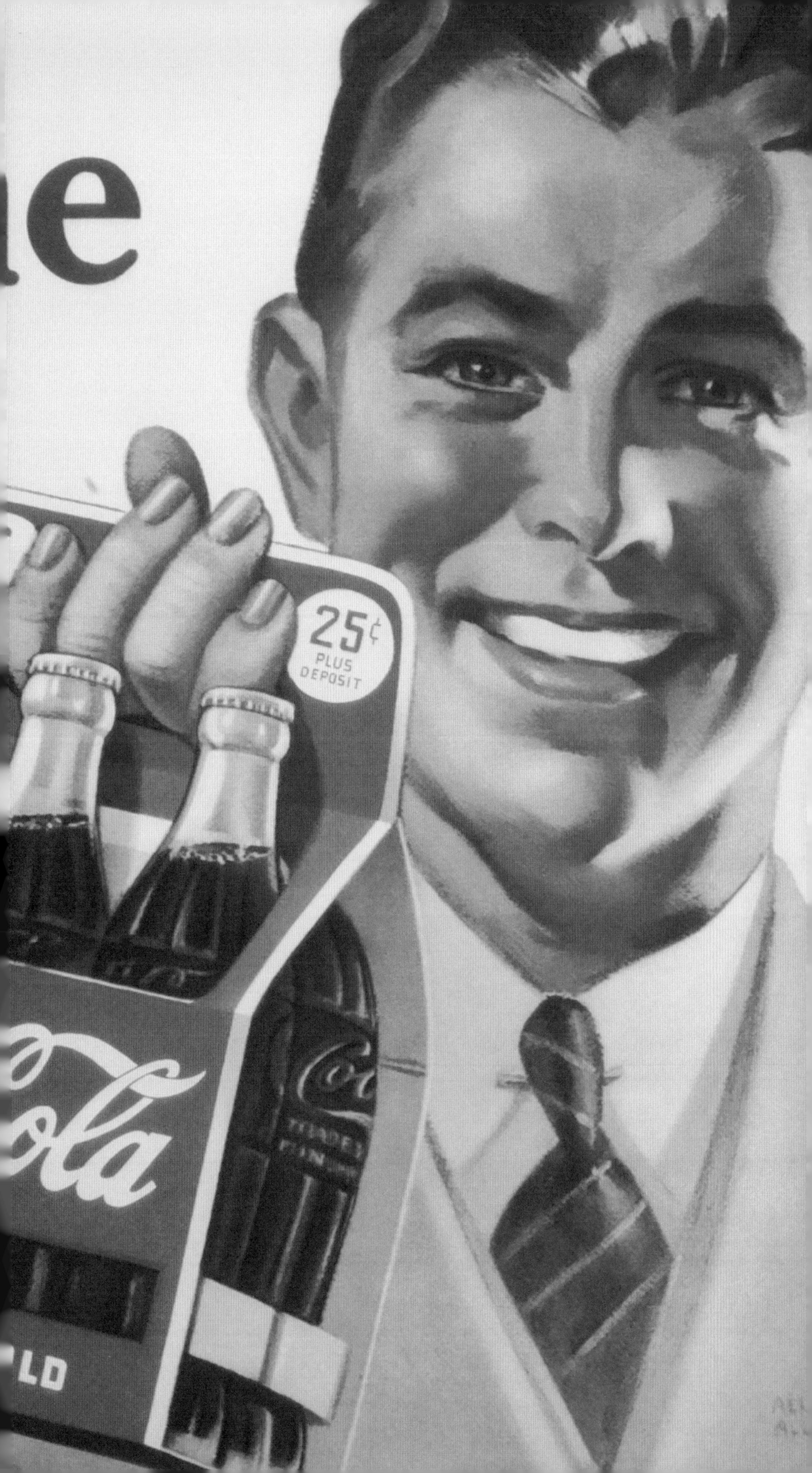

ne
25¢
PLUS
DEPOSIT
ola
LD

Sources and Acknowledgments

The main source of information for this book was the Coca-Cola Archives in Atlanta, Georgia, which provided internal documents, artifacts, images, and archived issues of company publications. For the general history of the company, this book relies on Frederick Allen's *Secret Formula: The Inside Story of How Coca-Cola Became the Best Known Brand in the World* (New York: Collins Business, 1994). Some Canadian context was provided by *All in Flavour*, an unpublished history by Howard Cash commissioned by the Canadian Soft Drink Association to mark its fiftieth anniversary in 1992. The genealogy resources of Ancestry.ca were employed to provide or confirm biographical details of many individuals profiled.

The book's team wishes to thank Canadian memorabilia collectors Ron Antonio, Bill Blake, and Bill Cook for their assistance and reminiscences. Our thanks also to historian Ted Ryan, archivist Jamal Booker, and Justine Fletcher, processing archivist and heritage communications, at Coca-Cola in Atlanta, for their advice and tireless labours.

At Coca-Cola Canada, thanks to Jamie Ferreira, Internal and Executive Communications Manager, Krista Scaldwell, VP, Public Affairs and Communications, and Megan Weait, Legal Counsel.

Beginnings
The profile of Charles Matson is drawn from genealogical sources. For information on Haliburton's Grand Central Hotel, see the Haliburton Highlands Museum website, http://www.haliburtonhighlandsmuseum.com/galleries/.
Information on J.L. Brissette derives from the company website, http://www.jlbrissette.com/equipe.html.

Thirst Knows No Season
Robert Woodruff's tour of western Canada, and his comments to a Los Angeles newspaper, draw on Frederick Allen's *Secret Formula*. The account of the Hambly brothers relies on Jennifer Weymark, "Memories of the Oshawa Arena," *The Oshawa Express*, Jan. 29, 2016. http://oshawaexpress.ca/memories-of-the-oshawa-arena/. The McLaughlin family's involvement with Canada Dry employs Howard Cash's *All in Flavour*.

Kelly's Team
All biographical materials derive from documents in the Coca-Cola Archives, except where Frederick Allen's *Secret Formula* is referenced.

Kosher Coca-Cola
The account of kosher Coca-Cola in Canada is drawn from documents in the Coca-Cola Archives. For the "koshering of Coca-Cola" in the United States in 1935, see Roger Horowitz, "The Real Thing: How Coke Became Kosher," *Chemical Heritage Foundation*, Fall 2012/Winter 2013. http://www.chemheritage.org/discover/media/magazine/articles/30-3-the-real-thing-how-coke-became-kosher.aspx.

Wartime

The account of Leo Couture draws on Andy O'Brien, "As a hockey executive, Couture is an oddity, because he was decorated for keeping mum," *Weekend Magazine*, vol. 9, no. 8 (1959), 48–49, and Baptiste Ricard-Châtelain, "Conférence de Québec de 1943: le point sur le J," *Le Soleil*, Aug. 13, 2013, http://www.lapresse.ca/le-soleil/actualites/societe/201308/30/01-4684902-conference-de-quebec-de-1943-le-point-sur-le-j.php.

For the Aboussafy family's arrival in Canada from Syria, see Vicky Lapointe, "Étiquette: Aboussafy," *Patrimoine*, Heritage et Multimédia, https://tolkien2008.wordpress.com/tag/aboussafy/. Details of Leo Aboussafy's life and Royal Bottling otherwise are drawn from genealogical sources and local newspaper accounts archived in Bibliothèque et Archives nationales du Québec.

In addition to an article in the January 1942 issue of *The Red Barrel*, the account of Norman Johnstone's experiences as a Spitfire squadron leader draws on *The R.C.A.F. Overseas, Vol. 1: The First Four Years* (Toronto: Oxford University Press 1944), 53–54, and Canadian Press, "Many Canadians Receive Awards in King's List," January 2, 1942.

The Movement to Youth

Biographical information on Bobby Curtola (who passed away while this book was being researched) derives from the singer's official website, http://www.bobbycurtola.com/.

Some details, including the quote attributed to Burton Cummings, on The Guess Who and the album *A Wild Pair* are found at Manitoba Music Museum, http://www.manitobamusicmuseum.com/theguesswho.htm.

We thank collector Bill Blake for his observations on the Hi-Fi Club in Canada.

"Let's Get Together/Salut Mon Frère"

The account of Olympic Games Montreal 1976 is based on materials in the Coca-Cola Archives. Athletic performances are drawn from records maintained by the Canadian Olympic Association.

The Community Bottler

MaryKay Melnyk, Michael Orser, and Janice Thompson shared memories of their father, Butch Orser. Bill Mackie and Daniel A. Dubeau provided reminiscences through a Facebook group dedicated to local history, in response to a posted request from researcher Douglas Hunter. The Pentanguishene Museum provided research materials related to the Moses family and the original bottling operation. Huronia Museum was a source of images and artifacts.

Spectacle and Society

The account of Coca-Cola's partnership with World Wildlife Fund in preserving polar bear habit draws in part on the article by Canadian Press, "Coke Changes Can, Offers Millions to Protect Polar Bears," Oct. 25, 2011, in *Marketing Magazine*, http://www.marketingmag.ca/brands/coke-changes-can-offers-millions-to-protectpolar-bears-38713.

For information on the character Max Headroom, see *The Max Headroom Chronicles*, www.maxhead-room.com.

Image Credits